WASHOE COUNTY LIBRARY

3 1235 01340 3451

P9-ECJ-744

FOR REFERENCE
DO NOT TAKE FROM THIS ROOM

NO LONGER PROPERTY OF
WASHOE COUNTY LIBRARY

POPULAR
MUSIC

The Popular Music Series

Popular Music, 1980–1989 is a revised cumulation of and supersedes Volumes 9 through 14 of the *Popular Music* series, all of which are still available:

Volume 9, 1980–84   Volume 12, 1987
Volume 10, 1985   Volume 13, 1988
Volume 11, 1986   Volume 14, 1989

Popular Music, 1920–1979 is also a revised cumulation of and supersedes Volumes 1 through 8 of the *Popular Music* series, of which Volumes 6 through 8 are still available:

Volume 1, 2nd ed., 1950–59   Volume 5, 1920–29
Volume 2, 1940–49   Volume 6, 1965–69
Volume 3, 1960–64   Volume 7, 1970–74
Volume 4, 1930–39   Volume 8, 1975–79

Popular Music, 1900–1919 is a companion volume to the revised cumulation.

This series continues with:

Volume 15, 1990   Volume 20, 1995
Volume 16, 1991   Volume 21, 1996
Volume 17, 1992   Volume 22, 1997
Volume 18, 1993   Volume 23, 1998
Volume 19, 1994

Other Books by Bruce Pollock

The Face of Rock and Roll: Images of a Generation

Hipper Than Our Kids?: A Rock and Roll Journal of the Baby Boom Generation

In Their Own Words: Popular Songwriting, 1955–1974

The Rock Song Index: The 7500 Most Important Songs of Rock and Roll

When Rock Was Young: The Heyday of Top 40

When the Music Mattered: Rock in the 1960s

ISSN 0886-442X

VOLUME 23

1998

POPULAR MUSIC

An Annotated Guide to American Popular Songs,
:luding Introductory Essay, Lyricists and Composers Index,
Important Performances Index,
Awards Index, and List of Publishers

BRUCE POLLOCK
Editor

The Gale Group

DETROIT • SAN FRANCISCO • LONDON • BOSTON • WOODBRIDGE, CT

Bruce Pollock, *Editor*

Gale Group Staff

Jolen Marya Gedridge, *Project Editor*
Mary Bonk, *Contributing Editor*
Pamela A. Dear and Michael Reade, *Contributing Associate Editors*
Rita Runchock, *Managing Editor*

Mary Beth Trimper, *Production Director*
Cindy Range, *Production Assistant*

Cynthia Baldwin, *Production Design Manager*
Barbara J. Yarrow, *Graphic Services Supervisor*

Theresa Rocklin, *Manager, Technical Support Services*
Charles Beaumont, *Senior Programmer/Analyst*

This publication is a creative work and fully protected by all applicable copyright laws, as well as by misappropriation, trade secret, unfair competition, and other applicable laws. The authors and editors of this work have added value to the underlying factual material herein through one or more of the following: unique and original selection, coordination, expression, arrangement, and classification of the information.

The Gale Group will vigorously defend all of its rights in this publication.

Copyright © 1999
The Gale Group
27500 Drake Rd.
Farmington Hills, MI 48331-3535

Library of Congress Catalog Card Number 85-653754
ISBN 0-7876-1507-2
ISSN 0886-442X

All rights reserved. No part of this book may be reproduced in any form, except for brief quotation in a review, without written permission from the publisher.

Printed in the United States of America

10 9 8 7 6 5 4 3 2 1

Contents

About the Book
and How to Use It

This volume is the twenty-third of a series whose aim is to set down in permanent and practical form a selective, annotated list of the significant popular songs of our times. Other indexes of popular music have either dealt with special areas, such as jazz or theater and film music, or been concerned chiefly with songs that achieved a degree of popularity as measured by the music-business trade indicators, which vary widely in reliability.

Annual Publication Schedule

The first nine volumes in the *Popular Music* series covered sixty-five years of song history in increments of five or ten years. Volume 10 initiated a new annual publication schedule, making background information available as soon as possible after a song achieves prominence. Yearly publication also allows deeper coverage—approximately five hundred songs—with additional details about writers' inspiration, uses of songs, album appearances, and more.

Indexes Provide Additional Access

Three indexes make the valuable information in the song listings even more accessible to users. The Lyricists & Composers Index shows all the songs represented in *Popular Music, 1998,* that are credited to a given individual. The Important Performances Index tells at a glance which albums, musicals, films, television shows, or other media-featured songs are represented in the volume. The "Performer" category—first added to the index as "Vocalist" in the 1986 volume—allows the user to see with which songs an artist has been associated this year. The index is arranged by broad media category, then alphabetically by the show or album title, with the songs listed under each title. Finally, the Awards Index provides a list of the songs nominated for awards by the American Academy of

About the Book and How to Use It

Motion Picture Arts and Sciences (Academy Award) and the American Academy of Recording Arts and Sciences (Grammy Award). Winning songs are indicated by asterisks.

List of Publishers

The List of Publishers is an alphabetically arranged directory providing addresses—when available—for the publishers of the songs represented in *Popular Music, 1998*. Also noted is the organization handling performance rights for the publisher—in the United States, the American Society of Composers, Authors, and Publishers (ASCAP) or Broadcast Music, Inc. (BMI); in Canada, the Society of Composers, Authors, and Music Publishers of Canada (SOCAN); and in Europe, the Society of European Songwriters and Composers (SESAC).

Tracking Down Information on Songs

Unfortunately, the basic records kept by the active participants in the music business are often casual, inaccurate, and transitory. There is no single source of comprehensive information about popular songs, and those sources that do exist do not publish complete material about even the musical works with which they are directly concerned. Four of the primary proprietors of basic information about our popular music are the major performing rights societies—ASCAP, BMI, SOCAN, and SESAC. Although each of these organizations has considerable information about the songs of its own writer and publisher members and has also issued indexes of its own songs, their files and published indexes are designed primarily for clearance identification by the commercial users of music. Their publications of annual or periodic lists of their "hits" necessarily include only a small fraction of their songs, and the facts given about these are also limited. ASCAP, BMI, SOCAN, and SESAC are, however, invaluable and indispensable sources of data about popular music. It is just that their data and special knowledge are not readily accessible to the researcher.

Another basic source of information about musical compositions and their creators and publishers is the Copyright Office of the Library of Congress. A computerized file lists each published, unpublished, republished, and renewed copyright of songs registered with the Office. It takes between six months and a year from the time of application before songs are officially registered (in some cases, songs have already been released before copyright registration begins). This file is helpful in determining the precise date of the declaration of the original ownership of musical works, but since some authors, composers, and publishers have been known to employ rather makeshift methods of protecting their works legally, there are songs listed in *Popular Music* that may not be found in the Library of Congress files.

Selection Criteria

In preparing the original volumes for this time period, the editor was faced with a number of separate problems. The first and most important of these was that of selection. The stated aim of the project—to offer the user as comprehensive and accurate a listing of significant popular songs as possible—has been the guiding criterion. The purpose has never been to offer a judgment on the quality of any songs or to indulge a prejudice for or against any type of popular music. Rather, it is the purpose of *Popular Music* to document those musical works that (1) achieved a substantial degree of popular acceptance, (2) were exposed to the public in especially notable circumstances, or (3) were accepted and given important performances by influential musical and dramatic artists.

Another problem was whether or not to classify the songs as to type. Most works of music are subject to any number of interpretations and, although it is possible to describe a particular performance, it is more difficult to give a musical composition a label applicable not only to its origin but to its subsequent musical history. In fact, the most significant versions of some songs are often quite at variance with their origins. Citations for such songs in *Popular Music* indicate the important facts about not only their origins but also their subsequent lives, rather than assigning an arbitrary and possibly misleading label.

Research Sources

The principal sources of information for the titles, authors, composers, publishers, and dates of copyright of the songs in this volume were the Copyright Office of the Library of Congress, ASCAP, BMI, SOCAN, SESAC, and individual writers and publishers. Data about best-selling recordings were obtained principally from three of the leading music business trade journals—*Billboard, Radio & Records,* and *Cash Box.* For the historical notes; information about foreign, folk, public domain, and classical origins; and identification of theatrical, film, and television introducers of songs, the editor relied upon collections of album notes, theater programs, sheet music, newspaper and magazine articles, and other material, both his own and that in the Lincoln Center Library for the Performing Arts in New York City.

About the Book and How to Use It

Contents of a Typical Entry

The primary listing for a song includes

- Title and alternate title(s)
- Country of origin (for non-U.S. songs)
- Author(s) and composer(s)
- Current publisher, copyright date
- Annotation on the song's origins or performance history

Title: The full title and alternate title or titles are given exactly as they appear on the Library of Congress copyright record or, in some cases, the sheet music. Since even a casual perusal of the book reveals considerable variation in spelling and punctuation, it should be noted that these are the colloquialisms of the music trade. The title of a given song as it appears in this series is, in almost all instances, the one under which it is legally registered.

Foreign Origin: If a song is of foreign origin, the primary listing indicates the country of origin after the title. Additional information may be noted, such as the original title, copyright date, writer, publisher in country of origin, or other facts about the adaptation.

Authorship: In all cases, the primary listing reports the author or authors and the composer or composers. The reader may find variations in the spelling of a songwriter's name. This results from the fact that some writers used different forms of their names at different times or in connection with different songs. In addition to this kind of variation in the spelling of writers' names, the reader will also notice that in some cases, where the writer is also the performer, the name as a writer may differ from the form of the name used as a performer.

Publisher: The current publisher is listed. Since *Popular Music* is designed as a practical reference work rather than an academic study, and since copyrights more than occasionally change hands, the current publisher is given instead of the original holder of the copyright. If a publisher has, for some reason, copyrighted a song more than once, the years of the significant copyright subsequent to the year of the original copyright are also listed after the publisher's name.

Annotation: The primary listing mentions significant details about the song's history—the musical, film, or other production in which the song was introduced or featured and, where important, by whom it was introduced, in the case of theater and film songs; any other performers identified with the song; first or best-selling recordings and album inclusions, indicating the performer and the record company; awards; and other relevant data. The name of a performer may be listed differently in connection with different songs, especially over a period of years. The name listed is the form of the name given in connection with a particular performance or record. Dates are provided for important recordings and performances.

Popular Music in 1998

Inveterate slaves to the pop music mainstream had to be extremely encouraged this year by a couple of developments, neither related to the quality of music, both having to do with the quantity and variety available to be heard by the masses—which has been an unresolved issue for most of this decade.

When *Billboard* magazine changed its Top 100 charts in late 1998, it was admitting that the great and grand old Top 40 rock/pop/R&B/country sound of several generations had long ceased to matter (as this page has certainly not been shy in noting), not only to purists and sentimentalists, but to record label and advertising executives. And that had to hurt. As if by wizardry, this new chart system ushered onto the Top 20 and thus onto pop radio a whole bunch of rock and roll guitar bands (and way too many country songs), in the process offsetting what had become a decade-long preponderance of dance, rap and hip hop hits.

Not entirely disconnected from the above move were the underground ripples also late in the year about a new delivery system for music in the wings. MP-3, consisting of Internet web sites containing free downloadable songs, is arriving just in time to fill an historic niche in the way the mainstream receives massive infusions of exciting (seemingly) new music. In the fifties, it was AM radio delivering the 45 to a starving pop-drenched throng. In 1965 or so, FM radio delivered the LP to the Rock generation. In 1981 MTV found a use for music videos and Total Coelo's "I Eat Cannibals" would define a hip uncharted territory for the masses to embrace. The CD soon followed, mainly so that everyone could replace their old LPs. It did nothing to relieve the narrowing range of music that descended upon the mainstream charts of the 1990s. Although much great music was still being made, less and less of it was been delivered to the masses, who don't get out too often and depend on the radio for its injection of the rock and roll spirit.

So, in line with this theory, MP-3, as the delivery system for the underground music of the Internet, would help create the new FM of FM radio, or, alternatively, an FMTV to MTV, bringing new (or at least largely unheard) songs and bands to the attention of mainstream radio, the catchiest of which would be able to find a place on the new *Billboard* charts! In the process, rock and roll would be saved! Again!

If this analysis engenders confidence toward the music of the millennium, the penultimate year of the current epoch had nothing to be ashamed about either, especially due to the flourishing of the hybrid genre long-touted in these pages: Middle of the Dirt Road.

Middle of the Dirt Road Flourishes

Lucinda Williams, easily this year's critical favorite, not only produced an album that many could take immediately to heart, but in doing so helped shape the predominant sound of 1998. Just off-off radio for most of the decade, gathering purpose and adherents, the countrified folk/blues rock amalgam of Middle of the Dirt Road came up with milestone after milestone this year. The author of "Passionate Kisses," a smash for Mary Chapin Carpenter in 1992, Williams re-released her own purer and rawer version of the song on one album, provided a standout track for the soundtrack of the movie *The Horse Whisperer* ("Still I Long for Your Kiss") and gave us numerous gems on her long-awaited new album *Car Wheels on a Gravel Road* ("Can't Let Go," "Right in Time").

Following her lead, the genre variously known as Triple A, Roots, Alternative Country, Americana, and other descriptive nomenclatures (but not quite so evocative as Middle of the Dirt Road), was more than equal to the task of filling the airwaves with music that mattered. The Billy Bragg/Wilco collaboration on the lyrics of Woody Guthrie was an event on a par with last year's re-release of the Smithsonian/Folkways boxed set of seminal country/blues/folk performances that influenced the musical tastes of the Sixties generation. By giving life to songs like "Walt Whitman's Niece" and "Way over Yonder in the Minor Key" (aided by the voice of Natalie Merchant), British folkie Bragg and Alt. Country avatars Wilco continued to extol the power of folk music, as espoused by its original poet laureate, Guthrie, deeply satisfying old fans of the music and awakening the ears of a new generation. This set the stage nicely for a re-evaluation of Guthrie champion and Folk demigod, Pete Seeger, whose songs, with the Weavers and as a solo performer, were celebrated by artists like Bruce Springsteen ("We Shall Overcome"), Greg Brown ("Sailing Down This Golden River"), Jackson Browne and Bonnie Raitt ("Kisses Sweeter Than Wine"), Nanci Griffith ("If I Had a Hammer") and Pete himself ("Where Have All the Flowers Gone") in *Where Have All the Flowers Gone: The Songs of Pete Seeger*. Meanwhile, Guthrie acolyte Bob Dylan, living off the acclaim of last year's critical rediscovery, had a year reminiscent of his 1960's heyday, with artists as varied as Eric Clapton ("Born in Time"), Sheryl Crow ("Mississippi"), Kenny Wayne Shepherd ("Everything Is Broken"), Phoebe Snow ("It Takes a Lot to Laugh, It Takes a Train to Cry") and Garth Brooks ("To Make You Feel My Love"), covering his album cuts and outtakes, both past and current. Dylan himself contributed "Dignity" to the TV soundtrack *Touched by An Angel* and "The Man in Me" to the movie *The Big Lebowsky*; the release of Dylan's legendary much-bootlegged 1966 live concert performance in England didn't hurt the burgeoning re-evaluation of the generation's premier folk hero. British cult item Robert Wyatt even paid tribute to the redoubtable troubadour with "Blues in Bob Minor" on his underground hit album *Shleep*.

Not to be slighted, Bob contemporary and competitor Phil Ochs gained a tribute album this year as well, highlighted by John Gorka's rendition of "Bracero."

Touted as the first of a long line of new Bob Dylans, Loudon Wainwright ("What Are Families For") justified the comparison further this year by duplicating Bob's feat of releasing an album during the same year as his son Rufus ("April Fools"). Then he went Bob one better by appearing along with his ex-wife, Kate McGarrigle, and Rufus, as well as other assorted friends and family in the much-respected *The McGarrigle Hour* ("Schooldays"), on which Kate resurrected her ineffably lovely "(Talk to Me of) Mendocino."

One of the last of the New Dylans, who eventually would spawn his own line of imitators, was Bruce Springsteen, whose new boxed set included many rare tracks ("Roulette," "Man at the Top," "My Love Will Not Let You Down," and the seminal "Thundercrack").

Other performers paid well-deserved tribute to the rich legacy of artists and songs that populate the vast Middle of the Dirt Road genre: Nanci Griffith (Guy Clark's "Desperadoes Waiting for a Train," Johnny Cash's "I Still Miss Someone," the Harlan Howard/Tompall Glaser classic "Streets of Baltimore"); Lyle Lovett ("If I Needed You" by Townes Van Zandt); Brooks & Dunn (Roger Miller's "Husbands and Wives"); Leon Russell (Merle Haggard's "Okie from Muskogee"), Tompall Glaser (Kinky Friedman's "Get Your Biscuits in the Oven and Your Buns in Bed"); Dwight Yoakam ("Rapid City, South Dakota," also from the Kinky Friedman tribute album); Willie Nelson (his own "My Own Peculiar Way"); Junior Brown ("Rock-a-Hula Baby," from the underrated Elvis canon); Linda Ronstadt (John Hiatt's "When We Ran," Bruce

Springsteen's "If I Should Fall Behind"); Rosanne Cash and K.T. Oslin remembered the recently deceased Tammy Wynette with "D-i-v-o-r-c-e" and "Your Good Girl's Gonna Go Bad," respectively. Tammy's own evergreen "Stand by Your Man" was posthumously re-released.

A new generation of Dirt Road performers joined the fray with their own eclectic choices. Country's latest darlings, the Dixie Chicks, unearthed an FM radio standard from Bonnie Raitt's first album, "Give It up or Let Me Go," as well as a forgotten classic from Tom Jans ("Loving Arms"). Made up of Richard Shindell, Lucy Kaplansky and Dar Williams, the one-off folkie supergroup Cry Cry Cry gave us a dozen reinterpretations of neo folk/country songs, led off by R.E.M.'s "Fall on Me." Blues diva Tracy Nelson continued her recent comeback by dusting off Lorrie Morgan's "In Tears."

Folk scene stalwart John Prine picked up a valued writer credit on the George Strait hit, "I Just Want to Dance with You," while newer hopeful Pierce Pettis cashed in with "You Move Me," as recorded by Garth Brooks. Nashville treasure Beth Neilsen-Chapman stoked her resume this year when Martina McBride revived "Happy Girl" and "This Kiss," which appeared in the movie *Practical Magic*, became a huge crossover hit for Faith Hill. Jim Lauderdale further established himself as one of country music's premier singer/songwriters ("I'll Lead You Home," "She Used to Say That to Me), while newcomer Allison Moorer quickly joined the ranks of quality writer/interpreters ("Alabama Song," and the Oscar-nominated "A Soft Place to Fall" from the movie *The Horse Whisperer*). From veteran bluesman Mose Allison ("Old Man Blues") to rookie wordslinger Dan Bern ("Tiger Woods"), the Middle of the Dirt Road was crowded with stellar songs, among then Vic Chesnutt's "Replenished," Richard Shindell's "Reunion Hill," ("Caleb Meyer" by Gillian Welch, Leslie Satcher's "Whiskey on the Wound" and "I Said a Prayer," both by Pam Tillis, Robbie Robertson's "Unbound" and Loreena McKennitt's surprising hit single, "Mummer's Dance."

Fans of Songs Rewarded

Fans of the well-crafted legendary song found sustenance in other more paved venues along the vaunted Information Highway of the 90's that stretched back miles and decades. Stopping in the 1960's, Beatle tunes abounded by Celine Dion ("Here, There and Everywhere"), Fiona Apple ("Across the Universe"), Junior Vasquez ("Come Together") and Goldie Hawn ("A Hard Day's Night"). A mother lode of treasures from that golden age was put forth in the boxed set *Nuggets: Original Artyfacts from the First Psychedelic Era* (which revived "Strychnine" by the Sonics, among seventy or eighty others). The Brian Wilson oeuvre expanded to include the rare "Soulful Old Man Sunshine" from 1969, found on the *Endless Harmony* soundtrack, as well as the brand new "Your Imagination" on his current solo album. Brian's duet with Tammy Wynette on "In My Room" was released on her tribute album. Titans of blues rock Jimmy Page and Robert Plant, erstwhile co-leaders of Led Zeppelin, got back together and managed to retain not only their audience but their massive chops ("Most High"). Ultimate 1960's popster Burt Bacharach continued to prosper; his album with unlikely collaborator Elvis Costello ("God Give Me Strength") was released and bands like Shonen Knife ("Raindrops Keep Falling on My Head") and Cockeyed Ghost ("Walk on By") found a way to bring him into the present, as did his old flame Dionne Warwick, who revived "What the World Needs Now Is Love" accompanied by the Hip-Hop Nation United.

Icons from the 1970's fared equally well. Stevie Nicks of Fleetwood Mac ("Landslide") continued her rocky comeback and Van Halen, the quintessential guitar band, not only released a new album ("Fire in the Hole") but were recipients of a tribute album as well (featuring "Jump" by Mary Lou Lord and "Why Can't This Be Love" by Gigolo Aunts). Youngsters, the Prissteens, fished Wreckless Eric's "I'd Go the Whole Wide World" out of the swamps of punk history, while Metallica made a hit out of Bob Seger's emblematic "Turn the Page." Rod Stewart looked to his own early 1970's past to resurrect the Faces standard "Ooh La La." It was thus the perfect year for the complete works of the Pink Faeries to be compiled (starring the oft-covered "Do It").

It was also the perfect year for Bette Midler to revive her reputation as an arbiter of past and future standards, with such choice selections as David Frishberg's "I'm Hip" from 1981 and "Boxing" by Ben Folds from 1995. Frishberg himself went even deeper into the back catalogue of antiquity for Harold Arlen's "Last Night When We Were Young," first made popular by Lawrence Tibbet in 1936. The year's Swing craze led a number of bands to explore eras past, among them the Royal Crown Revue (Arlen's "Stormy Weather" from 1933) and the Brian Setzer Orchestra (Louis Prima's "Jump, Jive and Wail" from 1956). Others chose to write their own original recreations ("Zoot Suit Riot" by the Cherry Poppin' Daddies). Rod Stewart made his move in the opposite direction as an interpreter, giving the benefit of his definitive voice to tunes written by people several decades his junior, dubbing them future classics in the process (Noel Gallagher's "Cigarettes and Alcohol," Ron Sexsmith's "Secret Heart").

Popular Music in 1998

But once again, no one had a better year as a songwriter than Diane Warren, who accounted for hits by artists in several genres, among them hip hop ("Have You Ever" by Brandy), country ("Just to Hear You Say That You Love Me" by Faith Hill and Tim McGraw), rock ("I Don't Want to Miss a Thing" by Aerosmith, from the movie *Armageddon*) and pop ("You Are My Home" by Vanessa Williams and Chayanne from the movie *Dance with Me*).

Movie Songs Predominate

These last two numbers reflect the further entrenchment of pop song usage as a necessity for successful moviemaking in the 1990's. Where the trailer has entered its MTV prime as a one minute marketing tool, more often than not it's a pop song that's up in the cab driving it. Perhaps the year's biggest soundtrack, aside from *Titanic*, which produced the inevitable "My Heart Will Go On" was *City of Angels*, which contained two Grammy nominated tunes, "Iris" by the Goo Goo Dolls and "Uninvited" by Alanis Morrisette. *Great Expectations* featured singles by an impressive roster of alternative acts, including Pulp ("Like a Friend"), Tori Amos ("Siren") and Scott Weiland of Stone Temple Pilots ("Lady, Your Roof Brings Me Down"). *The Prince of Egypt* assembled stars from virtually all genres of music. One of the best songs from that score was sung by bluegrass charmer Alison Krauss ("I Give You to His Heart"); undoubtedly the biggest coup of the project was the pairing of Whitney Houston and Mariah Carey on the Oscar winning "When You Believe." *Armageddon* had plenty of big guns beyond the headlining Aerosmith, including Chantal Kreviasuk (reviving John Denver's "Leaving on a Jet Plane") and Shawn Colvin (reviving Karl Wallinger's "When the Rainbow Comes"). In fact, as an enticement to cover a song, nothing beats movie soundtrack exposure (and the attendant big bucks). This year a new version of "For What It's Worth" was covered by Public Enemy and the writer, Stephen Stills, in *He Got Game*. Fiona Apple took on "Across the Universe" in *Pleasantville*. Ben Stiller and the gang serenaded us with "Build Me Up Buttercup" in *There's Something About Mary* (which also gave us the return of Jonathan Richman). The soul chanteuse Des'ree offered up Bruce Springsteen's "Fire" in *Hav Plenty*. Gordon Lightfoot's "If You Could Read My Mind," got a dance treatment by Ultra Nate and friends in *54*. Lauryn Hill crooned Frankie Valli's "Can't Take My Eyes Off of You" in *Conspiracy Theory*. The goofy *Baseketball* provided Reel Big Fish's take on A-ha's video age classic "Take on Me," while in the 1980's homage film the *Wedding Singer*, the Presidents of the United States revisited the beginning of the video age in "Video

Killed the Radio Star." Movie directors also have a pronounced flair for plucking obscure gems from the archives to beef up their film's veracity or to show off their acumen or merely to indulge themselves: for choice examples look no further than *The Big Lebowsky* ("Dead Flowers" by Townes Van Zandt), *Fear and Loathing in Las Vegas* ("Viva Las Vegas" by the Dead Kennedys), *Jackie Brown* (where film co-star Pam Grier revived her performance of "Long Time Woman," introduced in the 1971 film *The Big Doll House*) or *Rancho Deluxe* ("Livingston Saturday Night" and "Wonder Why We Ever Go Home" both by Jimmy Buffett, a couple of years before he ever put them on albums).

The Caroles, King and Bayer Sager, scored movie song success in 1998, once in a rare joint collaboration on "Anyone At All," sung by King in the movie *You've Got Mail*. Bayer Sager teamed up with David Foster on the Oscar nominated "The Prayer," sung by Andrea Bocelli and Celine Dion in the movie *Quest for Camelot*.

There's no underestimating the power of the right combination of song and movie. In fact, it was the performance of "You and Me and the Bottle Makes Three Tonight (Baby)" by Big Bad Voodoo Daddy in the 1996 movie *Swingers* that is credited with launching this year's infatuation with swing (along with the prominent placement of Louis Prima's version of "Jump, Jive and Wail" in a swingin' TV ad for the Gap).

TV's place in the post-MTV song dissemination process remained secure, with just about every weekly series of note having its own album of associated songs. Joining the ranks this year was the svelte and trendy *Ally McBeal*, a show whose clever usage of live performances by Vonda Shepherd ("Searchin' My Soul") and nostalgic oldies inserted for maximum impact ("Walk Away Renee") has elevated it to the forefront of his highly competitive field. Throw in a chubby fantasy baby dancing to the tune of "Hooked on a Feeling (Ooga Chaka)," and you almost have a hit single by the manufactured group Baby Talk. Another cult show with an album this year was the smarmy cartoon hit *South Park*, from which the aptly revised "Kenny's Dead" by Master P emerged, using variations on a theme by Curtis Mayfield from the one-time blaxploitation classic "Freddie's Dead." Realizing its power, superstars gladly accepted TV exposure. Diane Warren wrote "Love Can Move Mountains," which was sung by Celine Dion and God's Property on the *Touched By an Angel* soundtrack. Madonna contributed "Power of Goodbye" to introduce the hot teen show *Felicity*. The 1970's Cult hero Alex Chilton and his band Big Star collaborated with Ben Vaughn (composer of the music for *Third Rock from the Sun*) to update the tune "In the Street" for use on *That 70's*

xix

Popular Music in 1998

Show. Olivia Newton-John introduced "Love Is a Gift" on the soap opera *As the World Turns*. There was even a single noting the end of one of TV's greatest sit-coms, entitled "Goodbye Seinfeld."

No such history was made on Broadway this year. After an extremely successful 1997, few musicals left their mark on the ears of anyone other than their beleaguered backers in 1998. By far the year's biggest buzz was generated by the drag comedy *Hedwig and the Angry Inch* ("Midnight Radio"). As a songwriter, it was Stephen Sondheim who had the most activity, with a successful revival of his 1954 show *Saturday Night* by the Bridewell Theatre Company ("So Many People," "What More Do I Need"), a new recording of *Follies* (featuring "Can That Boy Fox Trot" by Ann Miller), and a cover of "If Momma Was Married" from *Gypsy* by Emily Skinner and Alice Ripley (of last year's lauded *Side Show*) in their new album *Duets*. Two more of last year's bumper crop of musicals issued cast albums, with *Triumph of Love* ("Teach Me How to Love You" by Betty Buckley and F. Murray Abraham) and *The Lion King* ("Shadowland") leading the way. Also of 1997 vintage, "Wheels of a Dream" from *Ragtime* received a cover from none other than Frankie Laine, a legendary crooner whose career started closer to the beginning of the century that musical celebrates than just about anyone else on the recording scene today. Looking a bit toward the future are the Bee Gees with their musical version of the movie *Saturday Night Fever* opening in England ("Immortality," which has also been covered by Celine Dion) and the ubiquitous Frank Wildhorn and his version of *The Civil War* ("Day the Earth Stood Still").

Women and Men

The Civil War in modern times, as played out on the battlefield of pop music, is more of a sexual than political one, with women claiming huge advances (both artistically and financially). The concept of The Lilith Fair, which started out as a tour featuring women-only, in 1998 symbolized much more than a mere event. Led by Fair organizer, Canadian singer/songwriter Sarah McLachlan ("Adia," "Sweet Surrender," "Angel"), women dominated the charts, awards nominations, and year-end polls as never before. Commercial superstars like Jewel ("Hands"), Alanis Morrisette ("Thank U") and Garbage ("I Think I'm Paranoid") brought customers flocking to the stores. Venerated idols and icons like Joni Mitchell ("Stay in Touch") and the Indigo Girls ("Scooter Boys") were accorded due reverence. In rock, Courtney Love's group Hole ("Celebrity Skin," "Boys on the Radio," "Playing Your Song") established their primacy with a fierce new record. Polly Jean Harvey continued her harrowing journey to acceptance ("Angelene," "A Perfect Day Elise"). Indie stalwart Ani DiFranco moved closer to mainstream adulation ("As Is," "Pulse"); Alana Davis hit the Top 40 with a version of "32 Flavors" from Ani's 1995 album *Not a Pretty Girl*. Sheryl Crow surprised many non-believers with a strong new work ("My Favorite Mistake"). Tori Amos did some of her best work since her striking debut in 1992 ("Jackie's Strength," "Raspberry Swirl"). The 1993's flavor of the month, Liz Phair, matured considerably in her 1998 effort ("Polyester Bride"). Newcomers to watch included Jonatha Brooke, formerly of the Story ("Secrets and Lies") and Patty Griffin ("One Big Love").

In this context, it is easy to miss the fact that for a few men, at least, music making is still a viable career goal, despite having no self-congratulatory tour to call their own. And despite having few magazines devoted to exploring their wants and needs, men proved equally adept at calling attention to some of their inner issues. The grand old man of the field this year was Eric Clapton ("My Father's Eyes"). Not surprisingly after his heart troubles, John Mellencamp was similarly reflective ("Your Life Is Now"). R.E.M., who lost their drummer due to health concerns, were hardly representative of alpha male proclivities ("Daysleeper"). Alternative heroes U2 chose 1998 to issue the rare ballad "Sweetest Thing." Again on the alternative front, Everclear were also caught up in family matters ("Father of Mine"). Collegiate thinkers the Ben Folds Five offered their brand of twisted empathy ("Song for the Dumped"), anti-folkie Beck reversed his stance ("Nobody's Fault but My Own"), Billy Corgan's Smashing Pumpkins were inordinately subdued ("Perfect," "For Martha"), and even diehard punks like Offspring had their sensitive moments ("Who Would Have Thought"). Oscar-nominated indie rocker Elliott Smith solidified his status as a brooding balladeer with a major label release ("Waltz #2"). Across a spectrum of anger men's feelings ranged from Pulp's bitter "This Is Hardcore" to the Verve's frustrated "Bitter Sweet Symphony" to the strikingly bluesy "Blue on Black" by Kenny Wayne Shepherd. The mournful sound of the late Jeff Buckley will be sorely missed ("Witches Rave"). Through it all, however, Pearl Jam stood solid ("Do the Evolution," "Wishlist"), Dave Matthews noodled along seemingly unconcerned ("Don't Drink the Water") and Scotland's underground faves Belle & Sebastian sustained their ironic whimsy ("Seymour Stein"). Offering the same kind of alternative to the touchy-feely side of the male ego as professional wrestling and horror films were groups like Rob Zombie ("Dragula"), Monster Magnet ("Space Lord"), Korn ("Got the Life") the indubitable Marilyn Manson ("The Dope Show") and the ineffable, indomitable Beastie Boys ("Intergalactic").

Popular Music in 1998

The Sound of the 1990's

Following in the Beastie Boys' racially-charged crossover tracks proved no easy task for this year's determined scenemakers. Just about the only one who accomplished it was Fatboy Slim aka Norman Cook, whose "The Rockafella Skank" was equal parts rant, rave, and tongue in cheek commentary on white "funk soul brothers." In the electronic dance arena mixmeister Tricky gave us Polly Jean Harvey on his own "Broken Homes." Closer to home, Linda Imperial dusted off Connie Francis' 1958 ode to summer break "Where the Boys Are," while the Bass All-Stars did a complete (and uproarious) renovation of Rupert Holmes' "Pina Colada Song," re-titling it "U Like Pina Coladas." Will Smith adapted the Bill Withers' classic "Just the Two of Us" to his own autobiographical ends. Rappers Lord Tariq and Peter Gunz were musically inspired by neighborhood heroes Steely Dan's "Black Cow" on the ultra urban "Deja Vu (Uptown Baby)," while Jay-Z crossed into the rarely traversed streets of Broadway past for some of "Hard Knock Life" from *Annie*, subtitling it "The Ghetto Anthem." Lauryn Hill clipped a chorus from Edie Brickell's "What I Am," for "A Rose Is Still a Rose," which she produced for Aretha Franklin. Her buddy in the Fugees, Pras Michel glommed the Bee Gees for "Ghetto Supastar," for the movie *Bulworth*. More typically, black groups continued to pay homage to classic white pop songs in the same time honored way of forebears like the Platters ("Smoke Gets in Your Eyes"), the Drifters ("White Christmas"), and the Marcels ("Blue Moon") of yore. There was Wyclef Jean's "Cheated (To All the Girls)," which bowed toward the Julio Iglesias ballad "To All the Girls I've Loved Before." Lauryn Hill covered Frankie Valli's "Can't Take My Eyes Off of You." Inoj gave us Cyndi Lauper's epic "Time After Time." Arguably the creater of this intriguing sub-genre, Sean "Puffy" Combs tried to do the landmark rock and rap merger achieved by Run-DMC and Aerosmith in the 1986 revival of "Walk This Way" one better with his own collaboration/tribute to Led Zeppelin ("Kashmir/Come with Me"). He failed.

Elsewhere on the mean streets of rap, trouble reigned ("Dangerous" by Busta Rimes). Parlaying their bad boy thug image into cold hard cash, rappers used sports metaphors ("I Got the Hook Up" by Master P, "Second Round K.O." by Canibus), gangsta references ("Still a G Thang" by Snoop Doggy Dogg) and party anthems ("The Party Continues" by Jermaine Dupri) to hide a deeper search for truth ("Money, Power & Respect" by the Lox, "Still Not a Player" by Big Punisher, "Father" by LL Cool J, "Goodbye to My Homies" by Master P). Yet positivity ruled in the world created by Lauryn Hill in her widely acclaimed album *The*

Miseducation of Lauryn Hill ("Doo Wop (That Thing)," "To Zion"). And the image of a new South arose proudly in the works of Atlanta-based OutKast ("Rosa Parks") and Goodie Mob ("Beautiful Skin"). Most positive of all was the return of Terry Callier ("Lazarus Man") after more than a decade away from music. His lush jazz-flavored soul/folk musings could create a sub-genre all their own.

Seven Days That Changed the Charts

On December 5, 1998, industry Bible *Billboard* magazine introduced their new Top 40 charts to the public. The product of much behind the scenes effort and soul searching, these charts performed at least one historic function. I haven't actually done the hours of research necessary to verify this, but it seems certain that the 26 country songs that occupied slots on the Top 100 of that week had to create a record as safely unbreakable as the one that Mark McGuire established on the baseball fields of America the same year. Except that this record was broken the following week, when 30 of the Top 100 tunes were country songs. Considering that of the top 100 singles of 1998, only four were country songs, this is a skewering of priorities even more massive than the elimination of 10 or 20 R&B tunes to make room for them. Will we continue to move in this direction in 1999 and beyond? While Shania ("You're Still the One") et al would surely hope so, I myself was much more encouraged by the sudden presence of more rock-oriented material like "Save Tonight" by Eagle Eye Cherry, "Fly Away" by Lenny Kravitz, "Lullaby" by Shawn Mullins, "Iris" and "Slide" by Goo Goo Dolls, "Inside Out" by Eve 6, Natalie Imbruglia's "Torn," "Pretty Fly (For a White Guy)" by the Offspring and "Never There" by Cake. This was more like the singles radio I remembered (and briefly re-experienced in 1993).

But even this potential feast could turn out to be a mirage and both the rock and country tracks could well be gone by spring thaw. A slave to teenage tastes, Top 40 is in the midst of a Baby Boom unheard of in this decade. Even with the aging Spice Girls ("Goodbye") in decline, there is still the ascendant Brittany Spears ("...Baby One More Time"), the nubile Monica ("The First Night"), the comely Brandy ("Have You Ever"), the super-duo of Brandy and Monica ("The Boy Is Mine"), the steamy Nicole ("Make It Hot"), the aspiring All Saints ("Never Ever"), the succulent Total ("Trippin'") along with the ubiquitous Missy Elliott). And there have probably not been as many hunky male harmony groups since the heyday of Dion & the Belmonts. You've got the Backstreet Boys ("I'll Never Break Your Heart"), 98 Degrees ("Because of You"),

'N Sync ("I Want You Back") and Five ("When the Lights Go Out"). Movie and TV-friendly Will Smith has made the cut ("Gettin' Jiggy Wit It") as a wily renegade uncle. The perennially fascinating Madonna is now the Auntie Mame of the genre, dispensing worldly secrets from behind her seven veils ("Ray of Light," "Frozen," "Skin"). In this context, the charming psychobabble of Barenaked Ladies ("One Week"), the valedictorian sentiments of Semisonic ("Closing Time"), the beery bravado of Fastball ("The Way") hardly stand a chance on a regular basis.

Keep tuned for the results. And if all else fails, there's always MP-3.

Bruce Pollock
Editor

A

Across the Universe (English)
Words and music by John Lennon and Paul McCartney.
Sony ATV Music, 1998.
Revived by Fiona Apple in the film and on the soundtrack album
  Pleasantville (Clean Slate/Work/Sony Soundtrax, 98).

Adia (Canadian)
Words and music by Sarah McLachlan and Pierre Marchand.
Sony ATV Music, 1997/Studio Nomado Music, 1997.
Best-selling record by Sarah McLachlan from the album *Surfacing*
  (Arista, 97).

Alabama Song
Words and music by Allison Moorer and Doyle Primm.
Windswept Pacific, 1998/Jae'wans Music, 1998/Farrenuff, 1998.
Introduced by Allison Moorer on the album *Alabama Song* (MCA, 98).

All I Want
Words and music by Amy Rigby.
Lympia Music, Hollywood, 1998/Chicksaw Roan Music, 1998.
Introduced by Amy Rigby on the album *Middlescence* (Koch, 98).

All My Life
Words and music by Joel Hailey and Rory Bennett.
EMI-April Music, 1997/Cord Kayla Music, 1997/Hee Bee Doinit, 1997.
Best-selling record by K-Ci & JoJo from the album *Love Always* (MCA,
  98). Nominated for a Grammy Award for R&B Song of the Year.

All the Places (I Will Kiss You)
Words and music by Aaron Hall and Manuel Seal.
Rickety Raw, 1998/Nate Love's, 1998/MCA Music, 1998/Jamron, 1998/
  BMG Music, 1998/Slack A. D. Music, 1998.
Best-selling record by Aaron Hall from the album *Let's Talk About Love*
  (MCA, 98).

Along Comes Mary
Words and music by Tandyn Almer.
Irving Music Inc., 1965.
Revived by Bloodhound Gang in the film and on the soundtrack album
Half Baked (MCA, 98).

Angel (Canadian)
Words and music by Sarah McLachlan and Pierre Marchand.
Sony ATV Music, 1997/Tyde, 1997.
Best-selling record by Sarah McLachlan in the film and on the
soundtrack album *City of Angels* (Warner Sunset/Reprise, 98).

Angelene (English)
Words and music by Polly Jean Harvey.
EMI-Blackwood Music Inc., 1998.
Introduced by PJ Harvey on the album *Is This Desire* (Island, 98).It is
an answer to Rick Cave's "West Country Girl".

Anyone At All
Words and music by Carole King and Carol Bayer Sager.
Lushmole Music, 1998/All About Me, 1998/Warner-Tamerlane Music,
1998.
Introduced by Carole King in the film and on the soundtrack album
You've Got Mail (Warner Sunset/Atlantic, 98).

April Fools (Canadian)
Words and music by Rufus Wainwright.
Rock and Roll Credit Card, 1998/Dreamworks, 1998.
Introduced by Rufus Wainwright on the album *Rufus Wainwright*
(DreamWorks, 98).

Are You Jimmy Ray
Words and music by Jimmy Ray and Con Fitzpatrick.
MCA Music, 1998.
Best-selling record by Jimmy Ray from the album *Jimmy Ray* (Epic,
98).

Are You That Somebody
Words and music by Timothy Mosley and Steve Garrett.
Warner-Chappell Music, 1997/Herbilicious Music, 1997/Black Fountain,
1997/Fox Film Music Corp., 1997.
Best-selling record by Aaliyah in the film and on the soundtrack album
Dr. Doolittle (Blackground/Atlantic, 97).

The Arms of the One Who Loves You
Words and music by Diane Warren.
Realsongs, 1998.
Best-selling record by Xscape from the album *Traces of My Lipstick* (So
So Def/Columbia, 98).

As Is
Words and music by Ani DiFranco.
Righteous Babe Music, Buffalo, 1998.
Introduced by Ani DiFranco on the album *Little Plastic Castle* (Righteous Babe, 98).

Ava Adore
Words and music by Billy Corgan.
Chrysalis Music Group, 1998/Cinderful Music, 1998.
Introduced by Smashing Pumpkins on the album *Ava Adore* (Virgin, 98).

B

...Baby One More Time (German)
English words and music by Max Martin.
Zomba Music, 1998/Grantsville, 1998.
Best-selling record by Brittany Spears from the album *Baby One More Time* (Jive, 98).

Beautiful Skin
Words and music by Craig Love, Robert Barnett, Thomas Burton, Cameron Gipp, and Willie Knighton.
C'amore, 1998/Goodie Mob Music, 1998.
Introduced by Goodie Mob on the album *Still Standing* (LaFace, 98).

Because of You (Danish)
English words and music by Anders Bagge, Aentor Birgisson, Christian Karlsson, and Patrick Tucker.
Air Chrysalis Scandinavia, 1998/Murlyn, 1998.
Best-selling record by 98 Degrees from the album *98 Degrees and Rising* (Motown, 98).

Better Than You
Words and music by James Hetfield and Lars Ulrich.
Creeping Death Music, 1998.
Best-selling record by Metallica from the album *Reload* (Elektra, 98).

Bitter Sweet Symphony (English)
Words and music by Mick Jagger, Keith Richards, and Richard Ashcroft.
ABKCO Music Inc., 1997.
Best-selling record by the Verve from the album *Urban Hymns* (Virgin, 97). Nominated for a Grammy Award, Rock Song of the Year, 1998.

Blue on Black
Words and music by Kenny Wayne Shepherd, Mark Selby, and Tia Sillers.
Music Corp. of America, 1998/Only Hit Music, 1998/Bro N' Sis Music,

1998/O/B/O Itself and Estes Park, 1998/Know Jack, 1998/JMM Music, 1998/Ensign Music, 1998.
Best-selling record by Kenny Wayne Shepherd from the album *Trouble Is* (Revolution, 98).

Blues in Bob Minor (English)
Words and music by Robert Wyatt.
Introduced by Robert Wyatt on the album *Shleep* (Thirsty Ear, 98).

Body Bumpin' Yippie Yi-Yo
Words and music by Feloney Davis, Euclid Gray, and Monica Gray. Smelzgood, Chicago, 1998.
Best-selling record by Public Announcement from the album *All Work No Play* (A & M, 98).

Born in Time
Words and music by Bob Dylan.
Special Rider Music, 1990.
Revived by Eric Clapton on the album *Pilgrim* (Duck/Reprise, 98).

Boulder to Birmingham
Words and music by Emmylou Harris and Bill Danoff.
Cherry Lane Music Co., 1975.
Revived by Emmylou Harris on the album *Spyboy* (Eminent, 98).

Boxing
Words and music by Ben Folds.
Fresh Avery Music, 1995/Sony ATV Songs, 1995.
Revived by Bette Midler on the album *Bathhouse Bette* (Warner Brothers, 98).

Boy with the Arab Strap
English words and music by Stuart Murdoch.
Introduced by Belle and Sebastian on the album *The Boy with the Arab Strap* (Matador, 98).

The Boy Is Mine
Words and music by Rodney Jerkins, Fred Jerkins, Brandy Norwood, LeShawn Daniels, and Japhe Tejeda.
EMI-April Music, 1998/Dean McTaggart, 1998/EMI-Blackwood Music Inc., 1998/Rodney Jerkins Music, 1998.
Best-selling record by Brandy and Monica from the album *Never S-A-Y Never* (Atlantic, 98) and from the album *The Boy Is Mine* (Arista, 98). Nominated for a Grammy Award, R&B Song of the Year, 1998.

Boys on the Radio
Words and music by Courtney Love, Eric Erlandson, and Melissa Auf der Mar.

Mother May I, Sherman Oaks, 1998.
Introduced by Hole on the album *Celebrity Skin* (DGC, 98).

Bracero
Words and music by Phil Ochs.
Barricade Music Inc., 1966.
Revived by John Gorka on the album *What's That I Hear: The Songs of Phil Ochs* (Sliced Bread, 98).

Breakdown
Words and music by Mariah Carey, Anthony Henderson, Charles Scruggs, and Steven Jordan.
Sony ATV Songs, 1997/Rye Songs, 1997/Krazyie Bone, 1997/Wish Bone, 1997/Steven A. Jordan Music, 1997.
Best-selling record by Mariah Carey from the album *Butterfly* (Columbia, 97).

Breakfast in Bed
Words and music by Loudon Wainwright.
Snowden Music, 1998.
Introduced by Loudon Wainwright on the album *Breakfast in Bed* (Virgin, 98).

Broken Homes (English)
Words and music by Tricky.
Songs of Polygram, 1998.
Introduced by Tricky featuring PJ Harvey on the album *Angels with Dirty Faces* (Island, 98).

Build Me Up Buttercup (English)
Words and music by Tony McCaulay and Michael D'Abo.
Warner-Chappell Music, 1969/EMI United Catalogue, 1969.
Revived by Ben Stiller in the film and on the soundtrack album *There's Something About Mary* (Capitol, 98).

Bye Bye
Words and music by Phil Vassar and Rory Bourke.
EMI-April Music, 1998/Phil Vassar, 1998/Rory Bourke, 1998.
Best-selling record by Jo Dee Messina from the album *I'm Alright* (Curb, 98).

C

Caleb Meyer
Words and music by Gillian Welch and David Rawlings.
Irving Music Inc., 1998/Cracklin' Music, 1998.
Introduced by Gillian Welch on the album *Hell Among the Yearlings* (Almo Sounds, 98).

Can I Get A...
Words and music by Shawn Carter, Irving Lorenzo, J. Atkins, and Rob Mays.
Lil Lu Lu Music, 1998/DJ Irv, 1998/Ja, 1998/EMI-Blackwood Music Inc., 1998.
Best-selling record by Jay-Z featuring Amil and Ja from the album *Hard Knock Life* (Def Jam/Mercury, 98).

Can That Boy Fox Trot
Words and music by Stephen Sondheim.
Herald Square Music Co., 1971.
Revived by Ann Miller on the album *Follies: The Complete Recordings* (TVT Soundtrax, 98).

Can't Let Go
Words and music by Lucinda Williams.
Lucy Jones Music, 1998/Warner-Tamerlane Music, 1998/Nomad-Noman Music, 1998.
Introduced by Lucinda Williams on the album *Car Wheels on a Gravel Road* (Mercury, 98).

Can't Take My Eyes Off of You
Words and music by Bob Crewe and Bob Gaudio.
Windswept Pacific, 1967/Seasons Four Music Corp., 1967.
Revived by Lauryn Hill in the film and on the soundtrack album *Conspiracy Theory* (TVT, 98). Featured on the album *The Miseducation of Lauryn Hill* (Ruffhouse/Columbia, 98).

9

Celebrity Skin
Words and music by Courtney Love, Eric Erlandson, and Billy Corgan.
Mother May I, Sherman Oaks, 1998.
Best-selling record by Hole from the album *Celebrity Skin* (DGC, 98).
Nominated for a Grammy Award, Best Rock Song of the Year, 1998.

Chances Are
Words and music by Bob Seger.
Hideout Records/Distributing Co., 1998.
Best-selling record by Bob Seger and Martina McBride in the film and on the soundtrack album *Hope Floats* (Capitol, 98).

Changed the Locks
Words and music by Lucinda Williams.
Lucy Jones Music, 1988/Warner-Tamerlane Music, 1988/Nomad-Noman Music, 1988.
Revived by Lucinda Williams on the album *Lucinda Williams* (Mercury, 98).

Cheated (To All the Girls)
Words and music by Wyclef Jean, Salaam Remi, Hal David, and Albert Hammond.
EMI-April Music, 1975/Casa David, 1975.
Revived by Wyclef Jean on the album *Carnival* (Ruffhouse/Columbia, 98).

Cigarettes and Alcohol (English)
Words and music by Noel Gallagher.
Creation Music, 1994/Sony ATV Songs, 1994.
Revived by Rod Stewart on the album *When We Were the New Boys* (Warner Brothers, 98).

Circle of Amour
Words and music by Prince Rogers Nelson.
Controversy Music, 1998.
Introduced by Prince on the album *Crystal Ball* (NPG, 98).

Closing Time
Words and music by Dan Wilson.
WB Music, 1998.
Best-selling record by Semisonic from the album *Feeling Strangely Fine* (MCA, 98). Nominated for a Grammy Award, Best Rock Song of the Year, 1998.

Clumsy (Canadian)
Words and music by Arnold Lanni and Michael Maida.
Sony ATV Music, 1998.
Best-selling record by Our Lady Peace from the album *Clumsy* (Columbia, 98).

Come and Get with Me
Words and music by Keith Sweat and Lee McCallum.
Keith Sweat Publishing, 1998/EMI Music Publishing, 1998/Wiz, 1998.
Best-selling record by Keith Sweat featuring Snoop Dogg from the
album *Still in the Game* (Elektra, 98).

Come Some Rainy Day
Words and music by William Kirsh and Bat McGrath.
Red Brazos, 1998/Kidbilly, 1998/Salzillo, 1998/Millermo Music, 1998/
Wanted Woman, 1998.
Best-selling record by Wynonna from the album *The Other Side* (Curb/
Universal, 98).

Come Together (English)
Words and music by John Lennon and Paul McCartney.
Northern Songs, Ltd., England, 1969/Maclen Music Inc., 1969.
Revived by Junior Vasquez on the album *Junior Vasquez* (Drive/Pagoda,
98).

Commitment
Words and music by Tony Colton, Tony Marty, and Bobby Wood.
Rick Hall Music, 1998/Monkids, 1998/Rio Bravo Music, 1998/
Congregation, 1998.
Best-selling record by LeAnn Rimes from the album *Sittin' on Top of
the World* (Curb, 98).

Corason De Oro
Words and music by Tim Armstrong.
Dr. Benway Music, 1998.
Introduced by Rancid on the album *Life Won't Wait* (Epitaph, 98).

Cover You in Kisses
Words and music by Jerry Kilgore, Brett Jones, and Jess Brown.
Ensign Music, 1998/Famous Music Corp., 1998/Divine Pimp Music,
1998/Jess Brown, 1998/Almo Music Corp., 1998.
Best-selling record by John Michael Montgomery from the album *Leave
a Mark* (Atlantic, 98).

Crazy Cries of Love
Words and music by Joni Mitchell.
Crazy Crow Music, 1998/Sony ATV Music, 1998.
Introduced by Joni Mitchell on the album *Taming the Tiger* (Reprise,
98).

Crown of Jewels
Words and music by Bruce Hornsby.
Basically Zappo Music, 1998/Warner-Chappell Music, 1998.
Introduced by Bruce Hornsby on the album *Spirit Trail* (RCA, 98).

Cruel Summer (English)
Words and music by Sarah Dallin, Siobhan Fahey, Keren Woodward, Tony Swain, and Steve Jolley.
In A Bunch Music, London, England, 1983/WB Music, 1983/Polygram International Music, 1983/Sony ATV Music, 1983.
Revived by Ace of Base on the album *Cruel Summer* (Arista, 98).

Crush (English)
Words and music by Andy Goldmark, Mark Mueller, Berny Cosgrove, and Kevin Clark.
New Nonpariel, 1998/WB Music, 1998/Be Le Be, 1998/About Time, 1998/Moo Maison, 1998/Almo Music Corp., 1998.
Best-selling record by Jennifer Paige from the album *Jennifer Paige* (Edel America/Hollywood, 98).

Crystal Ship
Words and music by Jim Morrison, Robbie Krieger, John Densmore, and Ray Manzarek.
Doors Music Co., 1967.
Revived by X and Ray Manzarek in the film and on the soundtrack album *The X-Files* (Elektra, 98).

The Cup of Life (Portuguese)
English words and music by Robi Rosa, Desmond Child, and Luis Escolar.
Draco Cornelius, 1998/Desmophobia, 1998/Polygram Music Publishing Inc., 1998.
Introduced by Ricky Martin on the album *Music of the World Cup* (Columbia, 98). This became the official theme of World Cup.

Cure for Love
Words and music by David Hidalgo and Louis Perez.
Hot Churro, 199 /Chicken on Fire, 199 .
Introduced by Bonnie Raitt on the album *Fundamental* (Capitol, 98).

D

D-i-v-o-r-c-e
Words and music by Bobby Braddock and Curly Putman.
Sony ATV Tree Publishing, 1968.
Revived by Rosanne Cash on the album *Tammy Wynette: Remembered* (Asylum, 98).

Da Bang
Words and music by Prince Rogers Nelson.
Controversy Music, 1998.
Introduced by Prince on the album *Crystal Ball* (NPG, 98).

Dangerous
Words and music by Rashad Smith, Trevor Smith, Henry Stone, Freddy Stonewall, and Lawrence Dermer.
T'Ziah's Music, 1997/Zadiyah's, 1997/Longitude Music, 1997/Warner-Tamerlane Music, 1998/Armacien Music, 1998.
Best-selling record by Busta Rhymes from the album *When Disaster Strikes* (Elektra, 98).

Day the Earth Stood Still
Words and music by Frank Wildhorn.
Introduced by Travis Tritt in the musical and cast album *The Civil War: The Nashville Sessions* (Atlantic Nashville, 98).

The Day That She Left Tulsa (in a Chevy)
Words and music by Mark D. Sanders and Steve Diamond.
Starstruck Writers Group, 1997/Mark D. Music, 1997/Diamond Three, 1997/Seven Summits, 1997.
Best-selling record by Wade Hayes from the album *When the Wrong One Loves You* (Columbia, 98).

Daydreamin'
Words and music by Rodney Jerkins, Fred Jerkins, Donald Fagen, Walter Becker, LeShawn Daniels, Peter Pankey, and Sean Hamilton.
Rodney Jerkins Music, 1998/EMI-Blackwood Music Inc., 1998/Ensign

13

Music, 1998/Bow Down, 1998/Gunz, 1998/Leshawn Daniels, 1998/
EMI-April Music, 1998/MCA Music, 1998.
Best-selling record by Tatyana Ali from the album *Kiss the Sky* (MJJ/
Work, 98).

Daysleeper
Words and music by Peter Buck, Mike Mills, and Michael Stipe.
Temporary Music, 1998/Colgems-EMI Music, 1998.
Best-selling record by R.E.M. from the album *Up* (Warner Brothers,
98).

Dead Flowers (English)
Words and music by Mick Jagger and Keith Richards.
ABKCO Music Inc., 1968.
Revived by Townes Van Zandt in the film and on the soundtrack album
The Big Lebowsky (Mercury, 98).

Dead Weight
Words and music by Beck Campbell, Michael Simpson, and Robert
King.
MCA Music, 1997/BMG Songs Inc., 1997.
Introduced by Beck in the film and on the soundtrack album *A Life Less
Ordinary* (London, 98).

Deja Vu (Uptown Baby)
Words and music by Donald Fagen and Walter Becker.
MCA Music, 1998.
Best-selling record by Lord Tariq & Peter Gunz from the album *Make It
Reign* (Codeine/Columbia, 98).

Delta Queen Waltz
Words and music by John Hartford.
Clement Family, 1972.
Revived by Van Dyke Parks on the album *Moonlighting* (Warner
Brothers, 98).

Desperadoes Waiting for a Train
Words and music by Guy Clark.
Warner-Chappell Music, 1973.
Revived by Nanci Griffith with Steve Earle, Jerry Jeff Walker, Jimmie
Dale Gilmore, Rodney Crowell, and Guy Clark on the album *Other
Voices, Too (A Trip Back to Bountiful)* (Elektra, 98).

Dignity
Words and music by Bob Dylan.
Special Rider Music, 1994.
Revived by Bob Dylan on the soundtrack album *Touched by an Angel*
(550 Music/Sony, 98).

Ding Dong Daddy of the D Car Line
Words and music by Steve Perry.
Famous Music Corp., 1994.
Revived by Cherry Poppin' Daddies on the album *Swing This, Baby* (Slimstyle/Beyond, 98).

Do the Evolution
Words and music by Stone Gossard and Eddie Vedder.
Innocent Bystander Music, 1998/Jumping Cat Music, 1998.
Introduced by Pearl Jam on the album *Yield* (Epic, 98).

Do It (English)
Words and music by Twink (pseudonym for John Adler).
EMI-Intertrax Music, 1971.
Revived by The Pink Faeries on the album *The Golden Years: 1969-1971* (Purple Pyramid/Cleopatra, 98).

Do for Love
Words and music by Tupac Shakur, Carsten Shack, Kenneth Karlin, Bobby Caldwell, and Jim Kettner.
EMI-Blackwood Music Inc., 1997/Heartworm, 1997/Hinayana, 1997/ Music Corp. of America, 1997/Parker Pen, 1997/Windswept Pacific, 1997/Music Force Pacific, 1997.
Best-selling record by 2Pac featuring Eric Williams from the album *R U Still Down (Remember Me)* (Amarij, 98).

Don't Drink the Water
Words and music by Dave Matthews.
Colden Grey Music, New York, 1998.
Best-selling record by The Dave Matthews Band from the album *Before These Crowded Streets* (RCA, 98).

Don't Laugh at Me
Words and music by Allen Shamblin and Ronnie Seskin.
David Aaron Music, 1998/Built on Rock Music, 1998/Sony ATV Cross Keys Publishing Co. Inc., 1998.
Best-selling record by Mark Wills from the album *Wish You Were Here* (Mercury, 98).

Doo Wop (That Thing)
Words and music by Lauryn Hill.
Sony ATV Music, 1998/Obverse Creation Music, 1998.
Best-selling record by Lauryn Hill from the album *The Miseducation of Lauryn Hill* (Ruffhouse/Columbia, 98). Won a Grammy Award for Best R&B Song of the Year, 1998.

The Dope Show
Words and music by Marilyn Manson (pseudonym for Brian Warner), Twiggy Ramirez, and Geordie White.

Dinger & Ollie Music, 1998/Bloody Heavy, 1998/Songs of Golgotha, 1998.
Best-selling record by Marilyn Manson from the album *Mechanical Animals* (Nothing/Interscope, 98).

The Down Town
Words and music by Travis Meeks.
Warner-Tamerlane Music, 1998/Scrogrow Music, 1998.
Best-selling record by Days of the New from the album *Days of the New* (Outpost/Geffen, 98).

Dragula
Words and music by Scott Humphrey and Rob Zombie.
WB Music, 1998/Demenoid Deluxe Music, 1998/Gimme Back My Publishing, 1998.
Best-selling record by Rob Zombie from the album *Hellbilly Deluxe* (Geffen, 98).

Dream Walkin'
Words and music by Toby Keith and Chuck Cannon.
Wacissa River Music, Nashville, 1997/Songs of Polygram, 1997/Tokeco Music, 1997.
Best-selling record by Toby Keith from the album *Dream Walkin'* (Mercury, 97).

Drift Away
Words and music by Mentor Williams.
Almo Music Corp., 1972.
Revived by Ringo Starr and Tom Petty on the album *Vertical Man* (Mercury, 98).

Driving My Life Away
Words and music by Eddie Rabbitt, Even Stevens, and David Malloy.
Screen Gems-EMI Music Inc., 1980.
Revived by Rhett Akins in the film and on the soundtrack album *Black Dog* (Decca, 98).

E

Everybody (Backstreet's Back) (German)
English words and music by Max Martin and Denniz Pop.
Zomba Music, 1998/Grantsville, 1998.
Best-selling record by the Backstreet Boys from the album *Backstreet Boys* (Jive, 98).

Everything Is Broken
Words and music by Bob Dylan.
Special Rider Music, 1989.
Revived by Kenny Wayne Shepherd on the album *Trouble Is* (Revolution, 98).

Everything's Changed
Words and music by Richie McDonald, Pete Nelson, and Larry Boone.
Five Cowboys, 1997/Sony ATV Tree Publishing, 1997/Terilee Music, 1997/Sony ATV Cross Keys Publishing Co. Inc., 1997.
Best-selling record by Lonestar from the album *Crazy Nights* (BNA, 97).

F

Faithful
Words and music by Stone Gossard and Eddie Vedder.
Innocent Bystander Music, 1998.
Introduced by Pearl Jam on the album *Yield* (Epic, 98).

Fall on Me
Words and music by Michael Stipe, Peter Buck, Mike Mills, and Bill
  Berry.
Night Garden Music, 1986.
Revived by Cry Cry Cry on the album *Cry Cry Cry* (Razor & Tie, 98).

Father
Words and music by James Todd Smith, Jean Claude Olivier, Samuel
  Barnes, George Michael, and Geoff Overbig.
Morrison Leahy, England, 1998/LL Cool J Music, 1997/Slam U Well
  Music, 1997/Jelly's Jams L.L.C. Music, 1997/Def Jam Music, 1997/
  Chappell & Co., Inc., 1998/Twelve & Under Music, 1998/Jumping
  Bean Music, 1998.
Best-selling record by LL Cool J from the album *Phenomenon* (Def
  Jam/Mercury, 97).

Father of Mine
Words and music by Art Alexakis, Greg Ecklund, and Craig Montoya.
Irving Music Inc., 1998/Evergleam Music, 1998/Common Green Music,
  1998/Montalupis Music, 1998.
Best-selling record by Everclear from the album *So Much for the
  Afterglow* (Capitol, 97).

Fire
Words and music by Bruce Springsteen.
Bruce Springsteen Publishing, 1979.
Revived by Des'ree in the film and on the soundtrack album *Hav Plenty*
  (Yab Yum/550 Music, 98).

Fire in the Hole
Words and music by Eddie Van Halen, Alex Van Halen, Mark Anthony, and Gary Cherone.
WB Music, 1998/Almo Music Corp., 1998.
Best-selling record by Van Halen from the album *Van Halen III* (Warner Brothers, 98).

The First Night
Words and music by Jermaine Dupri, Tamara Savage, Marilyn McLeod, and Pam Sawyer.
EMI-April Music, 1998/Dean Miller, 1998.
Best-selling record by Monica from the album *The Boy Is Mine* (Arista, 98).

Flagpole Sitta
Words and music by Evan Sult, Jeff Lin, Sean Nelson, and Aaron Huffman.
Famous Music Corp., 1998.
Best-selling record by Harvey Danger from the album *Where Have All the Merry Makers Gone* (Slash/London/Island, 98).

Fly Away
Words and music by Lenny Kravitz.
Miss Bessie, 1998.
Best-selling record by Lenny Kravitz from the album *5* (Virgin, 98).

For Martha
Words and music by Billy Corgan.
Cinderful Music, 1998/Chrysalis Music Group, 1998.
Introduced by Smashing Pumpkins on the album *Ava Adore* (Virgin, 98).

For What It's Worth
Words and music by Stephen Stills.
Ten-East Music, 1966/Cotillion Music Inc., 1966/Springalo Toones, 1966/Richie Furay, 1966.
Revived by Public Enemy and Stephen Stills in the film and on the soundtrack album *He Got Game* (Def Jam, 98).

Forever Love
Words and music by Liz Hengber, Deanna Bryant, and Sunny Russ.
Starstruck Writers Group, 1998/Glen Nikki, 1998/Starstruck Angel Music, 1998/Missoula, 1998.
Best-selling record by Reba McEntire from the album *If You See Him* (MCA Nashville, 98).

Friend of Mine
Words and music by Kelly Price, Steven Jordan, Jeffrey Walker, Anthony Dent, Jimmy Seals, and Dash Crofts.

Price is Right Music, 1998/Music Corp. of America, 1998/Steven A.
Jordan Music, 1998/Sony ATV Music, 1998/Dub's World Music,
1998/HGL Music, 1998/Warren G Music, 1998/Hit Co. South, 1998.
Best-selling record by Kelly Price from the album *Soul of a Woman*
(T-Neck/Island, 98).

From This Moment On (Canadian-English)
Words and music by Robert John Lange and Shania Twain.
Zomba Music, 1998/Loon Echo Music, 1998.
Best-selling record by Shania Twain from the album *Come On Over*
(Mercury, 98).

Frozen
Words and music by Madonna Ciccone and Patrick Leonard.
Webo Girl, 1998/No Tomato, 1998.
Best-selling record by Madonna from the album *Ray of Light* (Warner
Brothers, 98)

Fuel
Words and music by Kirk Hammett, James Hetfield, and Lars Ulrich.
Creeping Death Music, 1998.
Best-selling record by Metallica from the album *Reload* (Elektra, 98).

G

Get at Me Dog
Words and music by Damon Blackman, Samuel Taylor, and Earl Simmons.
Boomer X, Mt. Vernon, 1998/Ruff Ryders, 1998/Samuel Taylor, 1998.
Best-selling record by DMX featuring Sheek from the album *It's Dark and Hell Is Hot* (Ruff Riders/Def Jam/Mercury, 98).

Get Your Biscuits in the Oven and Your Buns in Bed
Words and music by Richard Friedman.
Ensign Music, 1973.
Revived by Tompall Glaser on the album *Pearls in the Snow: The Songs of Kinky Friedman* (Kinkajou, 98).

Gettin' Jiggy Wit It
Words and music by Will Smith, Samuel Barnes, Bernard Edwards, Nile Rodgers, Joe Robinson, James Alexander, Ben Cauley, Larry Dodson, Willie Hall, Harvey Henderson, Dave Porter, and Winston Stewart.
Bernard's Other Music, 1998/Treyball Music, 1998/Slam U Well Music, 1998/Jelly's Jams L.L.C. Music, 1998/Warner-Chappell Music, 1998/ Sony ATV Music, 1998/Warner-Tamerlane Music, 1998/Gambi Music Inc., 1998.
Best-selling record by Will Smith from the album *Big Willie Style* (Columbia, 98).

Ghetto Supastar (That Is What You Are)
Words and music by Pras Michel, Wyclef Jean, Barry Gibb, Maurice Gibb, Robin Gibb, and Russell Jones.
Gibb Brothers Music, 1998/Careers-BMG Music, 1998/Unichappell Music Inc., 1998/Warner-Tamerlane Music, 1998/Wu-Tang Music, 1998/Sony ATV Music, 1998/Tete San Ko Music, 1998/TCF Music, 1998.
Best-selling record by Pras Michel featuring Ol' Dirty Bastard and Mya from the film and on the soundtrack album *Bulworth* (Interscope, 98).

Give It up or Let Me Go
Words and music by Bonnie Raitt.
Kokomo Music, 1972.
Revived by the Dixie Chicks on the album *Wide Open Spaces*
(Monument, 98).

Give Me Forever (I Do)
Words and music by Carter Cathcart, James Ingram, Juni Morrison, and
John Tesh.
Tesh, Los Angeles, 1998/Yah Mo Publishing, Los Angeles, 1998/
Cartertunes, Cornwall, 1998/Juni Morrison, New York, 1998.
Best-selling record by John Tesh and James Ingram from the album
Grand Passion (GTP/Mercury, 98).

Given to Fly
Words and music by Mike McCready and Eddie Vedder.
Jumping Cat Music, 1998/Innocent Bystander Music, 1998.
Best-selling record by Pearl Jam from the album *Yield* (Epic, 98).

God Give Me Strength
Words and music by Burt Bacharach and Elvis Costello.
Feedbach Music, 1996/SMB, 1996.
Revived by Elvis Costello on the album *Painted from Memory*
(Mercury, 98). This was introduced in the 1996 movie *Grace of My
Heart*.

Gone Till November
Words and music by Wyclef Jean.
Sony ATV Music, 1997/Tete San Ko Music, 1997.
Best-selling record by Wyclef Jean from the album *Carnival*
(Ruffhouse/Columbia, 97).

Goodbye (English)
Words and music by Spice Girls, Richard Stannard, and Matt Rowe.
Full Keel Music, 1998/Windswept Pacific, 1998/Polygram International
Music, 1998.
Best-selling record by the Spice Girls from the album *Spice World*
(Virgin, 98).

Goodbye to My Homies
Words and music by Master P, Silkk the Shocker, Sons of Funk, Mo B.
Dick, Freddie Perren, and Christine Perren.
Big P Music, Baton Rouge, 1998/Burrin Avenue Music, Hollywood,
1998/Jobete Music Co., 1998/EMI-April Music, 1998.
Best-selling record by Master P featuring Silkk the Shocker, Sons of
Funk and Moe B. Dick from the album *MP Da Last Don* (No Limit/
Priority, 98).

Goodbye Seinfeld
Words and music by Richard Chambers.
Budget, 1998.
Introduced by Soda 7 (Jamie, 98).

Goodbye Song
Words and music by Jim Lauderdale and Harlan Howard.
Yah Yah Music, 1997/Mighty Nice Music, 1997/Hornbill Music, 1997.
Introduced by Jim Lauderdale on the album *Whisper* (BNA, 98).

Got the Life
Words and music by Korn.
Best-selling record by Korn from the album *Follow the Leader* (Immortal/Epic, 98).

Got You (Where I Want You)
Words and music by Adam Paskowitz, James Book, Nick Lucero, and Peter Perdichicizzi.
Cooch & Hooch, 1998/Ensign Music, 1998.
Introduced by The Flys in the film *Disturbing Behavior*. Best-selling record by The Flys from the album *Holiday Man* (Delicious Vinyl/Trauma, 98).

Grease 98 (English)
Words and music by Barry Gibb.
Gibb Brothers Music, 1978.
Revived by Frankie Valli (Polydor, 98).

H

Hands
Words and music by Jewel Kilcher and Patrick Leonard.
WB Music, 1998/Wiggly Tooth Music, 1998.
Best-selling record by Jewel from the album *Spirit* (Atlantic, 98).

Happy Girl
Words and music by Annie Roboff and Beth Neilsen Chapman.
Almo Music Corp., 1997/Anwa Music, 1997/BNC, 1997.
Best-selling record by Martina McBride from the album *Evolution*
  (RCA, 98).

A Hard Day's Night (English)
Words and music by John Lennon and Paul McCartney.
Northern Songs, Ltd., England, 1964/Maclen Music Inc., 1964.
Revived by Goldie Hawn from the album *In My Life* (Echo/MCA, 98).

Hard Knock Life (The Ghetto Anthem)
Words and music by Shawn Carter, Mark James, Charles Strouse, and
  Martin Charnin.
Lil Lu Lu Music, 1998/EMI-Blackwood Music Inc., 1998/45 Music,
  1998/Warner-Chappell Music, 1998/Instantly, 1998/Helene Blue,
  1998/MPL Communications Inc., 1998.
Introduced by Jay-Z on the album *Hard Knock Life* (Roc-A-Fella/Def
  Jam, 98).

Have a Little Faith in Me
Words and music by John Hiatt.
Careers-BMG Music, 1987.
Revived by John Hiatt on the album *John Hiatt's Greatest Hits* (Capitol,
  98). Nominated for a Grammy Award, Best Rock Song of the Year,
  1998.

Have You Ever
Words and music by Diane Warren.
Realsongs, 1998.

Best-selling record by Brandy from the album *Never S-A-Y Never* (Atlantic, 98).

Here, There and Everywhere (English)
Words and music by John Lennon and Paul McCartney.
Northern Songs, Ltd., England, 1965.
Revived by by Celine Dion on the album *In My Life* (MCA, 98).

Heroes (English)
Words and music by David Bowie and Brian Eno.
RZO, 1978/Screen Gems-EMI Music Inc., 1978/Careers-BMG Music, 1978.
Revived by The Wallflowers in the film and on the soundtrack album *Godzilla* (Epic Sony Soundtrax, 98).

He's Got You
Words and music by Ronnie Dunn and Terry McBride.
Sony ATV Tree Publishing, 1997/Showbilly, 1997/Warner-Tamerlane Music, 1997/Constant Pressure Music, 1997.
Best-selling record by Brooks & Dunn from the album *If You See Her* (Arista Nashville, 97).

History Repeating (English)
Words and music by Alex Gifford.
Chrysalis Music Group, 1997.
Introduced by Propellerheads with Shirley Bassey on the album *Decksanddrumsandrockandroll* (DreamWorks, 98).

The Hole
Words and music by Skip Ewing and James Hicks.
Acuff Rose Music, 1998/On the Mantel, 1998.
Best-selling record by Randy Travis from the album *You and You Alone* (DreamWorks, 98).

Holes in the Floor of Heaven
Words and music by Steve Wariner and Billy Kirsch.
Steve Wariner, 1998/Red Brazos, 1998/Kid Julie, 1998.
Best-selling record by Steve Wariner from the album *Burnin' the Roadhouse Down* (Capitol Nashville, 98). Nominated for a Grammy Award, Best Country Song of the Year, 1998.

Honey I'm Home (Canadian-English)
Words and music by Shania Twain and Robert John Lange.
Songs of Polygram, 1998/Loon Echo Music, 1998/Zomba Music, 1998.
Best-selling record by Shania Twain from the album *Come On Over* (Mercury, 98).

Hooked on a Feeling (Ooga Chaka)
Words and music by Mark James.

Screen Gems-EMI Music Inc., 1974.
Revived by Baby Talk on the album *Born to Dance* (Peter Pan, 98).

Horse Called Music
Words and music by Wayne Carson Thompson.
Wayne Carson, Los Angeles, 1998.
Introduced by Randy Travis on the album *You and You Alone* (DreamWorks, 98).

Horse and Carriage
Words and music by Cameron Giles, Samuel Barnes, and Jean Claude Olivier.
Killer Cam, 1998/Untertainment, 1998/Warner-Chappell Music, 1998/ Slam U Well Music, 1998/Jelly's Jams L.L.C. Music, 1998/Jumping Bean Music, 1998/Twelve & Under Music, 1998.
Best-selling record by Cam'Ron from the album *Confessions of Fire* (Untertainment, 98).

How Deep Is Your Love
Words and music by Rick Cousins, Tamir Ruffin, Warren Campbell, and Warryn Andrews.
Sony ATV Songs, 1998/Everyone Craves, 1998/North Avenue, 1998/ EMI-April Music, 1998/Nyrraw, 1998/Da Ish, 1998/Funky Noise, 1998/Famous Music Corp., 1998.
Best-selling record by Dru Hill featuring Redman from the album *Enter the Dru* (Island/Def Jam/Mercury, 98).

How Do You Fall in Love
Words and music by Randy Owen, Teddy Gentry, and Greg Fowler.
Maypop Music, 1998/Wild Country Music, 1998.
Best-selling record by Alabama from the album *For the Record: 41 Number One Hits* (RCA, 98).

How Long Gone
Words and music by Shawn Camp and John Scott Sherrill.
Shawn Camp, 1998/Foreshadow Songs, Inc., 1998/CMI America, 1998/ Sony ATV Tree Publishing, 1998/Nothing But the Wolf, 1998.
Best-selling record by Brooks & Dunn from the album *If You See Her* (Arista Nashville, 98).

Husbands and Wives
Words and music by Roger Miller.
Sony ATV Tree Publishing, 1966.
Revived by Brooks & Dunn on the album *If You See Her* (Arista, 98).

I

I Am Too
Words and music by Todd Snider and Will Kimbrough.
Mighty Nice Music, 1998/Music Corp. of America, 1998/I Heard Them, 1998/Will K, 1998.
Introduced by Todd Snider on the album *Viva Satellite* (MCA, 98).

I Can Do That
Words and music by Montel Jordan and Ted Bishop.
Hudson Jordan, 1998/Wixen Music, 1998/Mood Swing, 1998/Famous Music Corp., 1998.
Best-selling record by Montell Jordan from the album *Let's Ride* (Def Jam/Mercury, 98).

I Can Still Feel You (American-Canadian)
Words and music by Kim Tribble and Tammy Hyler.
Wildawn Music, 1998/Balmur Music (Canada), 1998/Brian's Dream, 1998.
Best-selling record by Collin Raye from the album *The Walls Came Down* (Epic, 98).

I Do (Cherish You)
Words and music by Keith Stegall and Dan Hill.
Smash Vegas, 1998/If Dreams Had Wings, 1998/Big Picture, 1998.
Best-selling record by Mark Wills from the album *Wish You Were Here* (Mercury, 98). Also recorded by 98 Degrees from the album *98 Degrees and Rising* (Motown, 98).

I Don't Want to Miss a Thing
Words and music by Diane Warren.
Realsongs, 1998.
Best-selling record by Aerosmith in the film and on the soundtrack album *Armageddon* (Columbia, 98). Nominated for an Academy Award, Best Song of the Year, 1998.

I Get Lonely
Words and music by James III Harris, Terry Lewis, and Janet Jackson.
EMI-April Music, 1998/Flyte Tyme Tunes, 1998/Genro's Mood, 1998.
Best-selling record by Janet Jackson from the album *The Velvet Rope* (Virgin, 97).

I Give You to His Heart
Words and music by Ron Block.
Moonlight Canyon, 1998/Bug Music, 1998.
Introduced by Alison Krauss in the film and on the soundtrack album *The Prince of Egypt* (DreamWorks, 98).

I Got the Hook Up
Words and music by Master P and Sons of Funk.
Big P Music, Baton Rouge, 1998/Burrin Avenue Music, Hollywood, 1998.
Best-selling record by Master P featuring Sons of Funk from the album *MP da Last Don* (No Limit/Priority, 98).

I Honestly Love You (American-Australian)
Words and music by Peter Allen and Jeff Barry.
Irving Music Inc., 1974/Jeff Barry Music, 1974/Woolnough Music Inc., 1984.
Revived by Olivia Newton-John on the album *Back with a Heart* (MCA, 98).

I Just Want to Dance with You
Words and music by Roger Cook and John Prine.
Big Ears Music Inc., 1998/Bruised Oranges, 1998/Bug Music, 1998/ Screen Gems-EMI Music Inc., 1998.
Best-selling record by George Strait from the album *One Step at a Time* (MCA Nashville, 98).

I Lie in the Bed I Made
Words and music by Daron Johnson and Marti Frederiksen.
Virgin Music, 1998/Heathalee, 1998/Pearl White, 1998.
Best-selling record by Brother Cane from the album *Wishpool* (Virgin, 98).

I Only Wanna Be with You (English)
Words and music by Mike Hawker and Ivor Raymonde.
Springfield Music Ltd., London, England, 1963/Chappell & Co., Inc., 1963.
Revived by Vonda Shepherd in the TV show Ally McBeal and on the soundtrack album *Songs from Ally McBeal* (550 Music, 98).

I Said a Prayer
Words and music by Leslie Satcher.
EMI-Blackwood Music Inc., 1998/Song Island Music, 1998.

Best-selling record by Pam Tillis from the album *Every Time* (Arista Nashville, 98).

I Still Believe (Italian)
English words and music by Antonina Armato and Guiseppe Cantarelli.
Camex Music Inc., 1988/Colgems-EMI Music, 1988/Tom Sturges, 1988.
Revived by Mariah Carey on the album *#1's* (Columbia, 98).

I Still Love You
Words and music by Tony Tolbert, Darren Lighty, Robert Huggar, Raphael Brown, Arkieda Clowers, Johnny Bristol, and Kenny Edmunds.
EMI-April Music, 1998/TJ, 1998/Hank Linderman, 1998/Sony ATV Music, 1998/Hip Chic, 1998/WB Music, 1998/Bipa, 1998/Do What I Gotta Music, 1998.
Best-selling record by Next from the album *Rated Next* (Arista, 97).

I Still Miss Someone
Words and music by Johnny Cash and Roy Cash.
House of Cash Inc., 1958/Southwind Music, Inc., 1958/Unichappell Music Inc., 1958.
Revived by Nanci Griffith on the album *Other Voices, Too (A Trip Back to Bountiful)* (Elektra, 98).

I Think I Love You
Words and music by Tony Romeo.
Screen Gems-EMI Music Inc., 1970.
Revived by David Cassidy on the album *Old Trick, New Dog* (Slamajama, 98).

I Think I'm Paranoid
Words and music by Duke Erickson, Shirley Manson, Butch Vig, and Steve Marker.
Irving Music Inc., 1998/Vibe Crusher Music, 1998.
Best-selling record by Garbage from the album *Garbage Version 2.0* (Almo Sounds/Interscope, 98).

I Wanna Fall in Love
Words and music by Mark Spiro and Buddy Brook.
M. Spiro, 1997/Hidden Words, 1997/Acuff Rose Music, 1997.
Best-selling record by Lila McCann from the album *Lila* (Asylum, 97).

I Want to Spend My Lifetime Loving You
Words and music by James Horner and Will Jennings.
Introduced by Marc Anthony and Tina Arena in the film *The Mask of Zorro* (Sony Classics/Sony Soundtrax, 98).

I Want You Back (German)
English words and music by Max Martin and Denniz Pop.

Cheiron Music, 1998/BMG Music, 1998.
Best-selling record by 'N Sync from the album *'N Sync* (RCA, 98).

I Will Buy You a New Life
Words and music by Art Alexakis, Greg Ecklund, and Carlos Montoya.
Irving Music Inc., 1998/Evergleam Music, 1998/Common Green Music, 1998/Montalupis Music, 1998.
Best-selling record by Everclear from the album *So Much for the Afterglow* (Capitol, 97).

I Will Wait
Words and music by Mark Bryan, Darius Rucker, Jim Sonnefeld, and Dean Felber.
EMI-April Music, 1998/Monica's Reluctance to Lob, 1998.
Best-selling record by Hootie & the Blowfish from the album *Musical Chairs* (Atlantic, 98).

I'd Go the Whole Wide World (English)
Words and music by Eric Goulden.
Zomba Music, 1978.
Revived by The Prissteens on the album *Scandal, Controversy & Romance* (Almo Sounds, 98).

If I Had a Hammer
Words and music by Pete Seeger and Lee Hayes.
Ludlow Music Inc., 1958.
Revived by Nanci Griffith from the album *Where Have All the Flowers Gone: The Songs of Pete Seeger* (Appleseed/Red House, 98).

If I Needed You
Words and music by Townes Van Zandt.
EMI U Catalogue, 1972.
Revived by Lyle Lovett on the album *Step Inside This House* (Curb/ MCA, 98).

If I Never Stop Loving You
Words and music by Donny Kees and Skip Ewing.
Acuff Rose Music, 1997.
Best-selling record by David Kersh from the album *If I Never Stop Loving You* (Curb, 98).

If I Should Fall Behind
Words and music by Bruce Springsteen.
Bruce Springsteen Publishing, 1992.
Revived by Linda Ronstadt on the album *We Ran* (Elektra, 98).

If Momma Was Married
Words and music by Stephen Sondheim and Jule Styne.
Stratford Music Corp., 1959/Williamson Music, 1959.

Revived by Emily Skinner and Alice Ripley on the album *Duets* (Varese Sarabande, 98).

If You Could Read My Mind (Canadian)
Words and music by Gordon Lightfoot.
Early Morning Music, 1974.
Revived by Stars on 54: Ultra Nate, Amber, and Joceyln Enriquez in the film and on the soundtrack album *54* (Tommy Boy, 98).

If You Ever Did Believe
Words and music by Stevie Nicks.
Welsh Witch Publishing, 1998/Sony ATV Songs, 1998.
Introduced by Stevie Nicks in the film and on the soundtrack album *Practical Magic* (Warner Sunset/Reprise, 98).

If You Ever Have Forever in Mind
Words and music by Vince Gill and Troy Seals.
Benefit Music, 1998/Irving Music Inc., 1998/Baby Dumplin', 1998.
Best-selling record by Vince Gill from the album *The Key* (MCA Nashville, 98). Nominated for a Grammy Award, Best Country Song of the Year, 1998.

If You See Him/If You See Her
Words and music by Tommy Lee James, Jennifer Kimball, and Terry McBride.
Still Working for the Man Music, 1998/Songs of Polygram, 1998/EMI-Blackwood Music Inc., 1998/Garden Angel, 1998/Warner-Tamerlane Music, 1998/Constant Pressure Music, 1998.
Best-selling record by Reba McEntire and Brooks & Dunn from the album *If You See Her* (Arista Nashville, 98) and *If You See Him* (MCA Nashville, 98).

I'll Be
Words and music by Edwin McCain.
EMI-April Music, 1998/Farm Hand, 1998.
Best-selling record by Edwin McCain from the album *Misguided Roses* (Lava/Atlantic, 98).

I'll Dip
Words and music by Dallas Austin.
D.A.R.P. Music, 1998/EMI-April Music, 1998.
Introduced by Aretha Franklin on the album *A Rose Is Still a Rose* (Arista, 98).

I'll Go on Loving You
Words and music by Kieran Kane.
Spur66, 1998/Moraine, 1998/Little Duck, 1998.
Best-selling record by Alan Jackson from the album *I'll Go on Loving You* (Arista Nashville, 98).

I'll Lead You Home
Words and music by Jim Lauderdale.
Hornbill Music, 1998/Mighty Nice Music, 1998.
Introduced by Jim Lauderdale on the album *Whisper* (BNA, 98).

I'll Never Break Your Heart
Words and music by Eugene Wilde and Albert Manno.
Zomba Music, 1996/Dujuan, 1996/ECG, 1996.
Best-selling record by Backstreet Boys from the album *Backstreet Boys* (Jive, 96).

I'll Think of a Reason Later
Words and music by Tony Martin and Tim Nichols.
Hamstein Cumberland, Nashville, 1998/Baby Mae Music, Austin, 1998/ EMI-Blackwood Music Inc., 1998/Tyland Music, 1998.
Introduced by Lee Ann Womack on the album *Some Things I Know* (Decca, 98).

I'm Alright
Words and music by Phil Vassar.
EMI-April Music, 1998/Phil Vassar, 1998.
Best-selling record by Jo Dee Messina from the album *I'm Alright* (Curb, 98).

I'm from the Country
Words and music by Marty Brown, Richard Young, and Stan Webb.
Bug Music, 1998/High and Dry, 1998/Them Young Boys, 1998/Stan Webb, 1998.
Best-selling record by Tracy Byrd from the album *I'm from the Country* (MCA Nashville, 98).

I'm Hip
Words and music by David Frishberg and Bob Dorough.
Almo Music Corp., 1981/Kohaw, 1981.
Revived by Bette Midler on the album *Bathhouse Bette* (Warner Brothers, 98).

I'm So Happy I Can't Stop Crying (English)
Words and music by Sting (pseudonym for Gordon Sumner).
EMI-Blackwood Music Inc., 1997.
Best-selling record by Toby Keith with Sting from the album *Dream Walkin'* (Mercury, 97).

I'm Your Angel
Words and music by Robert Kelly.
Zomba Music, 1998/R. Kelly Music, 1998.
Best-selling record by R. Kelly and Celine Dion from the album *R* (Jive, 98). Also on the album *These Are Special Times* (550 Music, 98).

Imagination
Words and music by Jermaine Dupri, Manuel Seal, Berry Gordy, Fonze Mizell, Freddie Perren, and Deke Richards.
EMI-April Music, 1998/BMG Songs Inc., 1998/Jobete Music Co., 1998.
Best-selling record by Tamia from the album *Tamia* (Qwest/Warner Brothers, 98).

Imagine That
Words and music by William George, John Tirro, and Bryan White.
Seventh Son Music, 1997/New Haven Music, 1997.
Best-selling record by Diamond Rio from the album *Unbelievable* (Arista Nashville, 97).

Immortality (English)
Words and music by Barry Gibb, Robin Gibb, and Maurice Gibb.
Gibb Brothers Music, 1998.
Introduced by Celine Dion on the album *Let's Talk About Love* (Epic, 9?). Revived by Adam Garcia in the musical *Saturday Night Fever*.

In My Room
Words and music by Brian Wilson and Gary Usher.
Irving Music Inc., 1964.
Revived by Brian Wilson and Tammy Wynette on the album *Tammy Wynette Remembered* (Asylum, 98).

In the Street
Words and music by Alex Chilton, Chris Bell, and Ben Vaughn.
Almo Music Corp., 1972/Koala Music Inc., 1972.
Revived by Big Star in the TV series *That 70's Show*.

In Tears
Words and music by Mike Reid and Rory Bourke.
Chappell & Co., Inc., 1991/BMG Songs Inc., 1991.
Revived by Tracy Nelson on the album *Sing It* (Rounder, 98).

Inside Out
Words and music by Max Collins, James Fagenson, and Jonathan Siebels.
Less Than Zero, 1998/Fake and Jaded, 1998/Southfield Road, 1998.
Best-selling record by Eve 6 from the album *Eve 6* (RCA, 98).

Intergalactic
Words and music by Beastie Boys and Mario Caldato, Jr.
Brooklyn Dust Music, 1998/Polygram International Music, 1998.
Best-selling record by the Beastie Boys from the album *Hello Nasty* (Grand Royal/Capitol, 98).

Invisible Sun (English)
Words and music by Sting (pseudonym for Gordon Sumner).

EMI-Blackwood Music Inc., 1981.
Revived by Sting and Aswad in the film and on the soundtrack album
The X-Files (Elektra, 97).

Iris
Words and music by John Rzeznik.
Virgin Music, 1997/Scrap Metal Music, 1997.
Best-selling record by Goo Goo Dolls from the album *Dizzy Up the Girl*
(Warner Brothers, 98). From the movie *City of Angels*. Nominated for
a Grammy Award, Best Song of the Year, 1998.

Is Heaven Good Enough for You
Words and music by Doyle Primm and Allison Moorer.
World Pacific, 1998/Louise Red, 1998/Full Pull, 1998.
Introduced by Alison Moorer on the album *Alabama Song* (MCA
Nashville, 98).

It Must Be Love
Words and music by Craig Bickhardt and Jack Sundrun.
Almo Music Corp., 1998/Craig Bickhardt Music, 1998/Magnasong,
1998/Red Quill, 1998.
Best-selling record by Ty Herndon from the album *Big Hopes* (Epic,
98).

It Takes a Lot to Laugh, It Takes a Train to Cry
Words and music by Bob Dylan.
Special Rider Music, 1966.
Revived by Phoebe Snow on the album *I Can't Complain* (House of
Blues/Platinum, 98).

It Would Be You
Words and music by Kent Robbins and Dana Oglesby.
Colter Bay Music, 1998/Irving Music Inc., 1998/Neon Sky Music, 1998.
Best-selling record by Gary Allen from the album *It Would Be You*
(Decca, 98).

It's All About Me
Words and music by Daryl Pearson, Mark Andrews, Anne Dudley,
Trevor Horn, Jonathan Jeczalic, Gary Langan, and Paul Morley.
D'extraordinary, 1998/Warner-Chappell Music, 1998/Urban Warfare,
1998/WB Music, 1998/SPZ, 1998/Perfect Songs Music, 1998.
Best-selling record by Mya with special guest Sisqo from the album
Mya (University/Interscope, 98).

It's Alright
Words and music by Peter Klett, Dave Krusin, Bardi Martin, and Kevin
Martin.
Skinny White Butt, 1998/WB Music, 1998.

Best-selling record by Candlebox from the album *Happy Pills* (Maverick/Reprise, 98).

It's Your Song
Words and music by Benita Hill and Pamela Wolfe.
Gooby, 1998/Pan for Gold, 1998/Copyright Management Inc., 1998.
Best-selling record by Garth Brooks from the album *Double Live* (Capitol, 98).

J

Jackie's Strength
Words and music by Tori Amos.
Sword and Stone Music, 1998.
Introduced by Tori Amos on the album *From the Choirgirl Hotel*
(Atlantic, 98).

Jump
Words and music by Eddie Van Halen, Alex Van Halen, Mark Anthony,
and David Lee Roth.
WB Music, 1984.
Revived by Mary Lou Lord on the album *Everybody Wants Some: A
Loose Interpretation of the Musical Genius of Van Halen*
(CherryDisc/Roadrunner, 98).

Jump, Jive and Wail
Words and music by Louis Prima.
Larry Spier, Inc., 1956.
Revived by The Brian Setzer Orchestra on the album *The Dirty Boogie*
(Interscope, 98).

Jumper
Words and music by Stephan Jenkins, Kevin Cadogan, Brad Hargreaves,
and Arion Salazar.
EMI-Blackwood Music Inc., 1997/3EB Music, 1997.
Best-selling record by Third Eye Blind from the album *Third Eye Blind*
(Elektra, 97).

Just to Hear You Say That You Love Me
Words and music by Diane Warren.
Realsongs, 1998.
Best-selling record by Faith Hill with Tim McGraw from the album
Faith (Warner Brothers, 98).

Just to See You Smile
Words and music by Mark Nesler and Tony Martin.

Hamstein Cumberland, Nashville, 1997/Baby Mae Music, Austin, 1997/ Music Corp. of America, 1997/Glitterfish, 1997.
Best-selling record by Tim McGraw from the album *Everywhere* (Curb, 97).

Just the Two of Us
Words and music by Will Smith, Bill Withers, William Salter, and Ralph McDonald.
Antisia Music Inc., 1998/TCF, 1998.
Best-selling record by Will Smith from the album *Big Willie Style* (Columbia, 98).

K

Karma Police (English)
Words and music by Jonathan Greenwood, Phillip Selway, Edward
O'Brien, Thomas Yorke, and Colin Greenwood.
WB Music, 1997.
Best-selling record by Radiohead from the album *OK Computer*
(Capitol, 97).

Kashmir/Come with Me (English)
Words and music by Jimmy Page, Robert Plant, John Paul Jones, Sean
Combs, and Mark Curry.
Flames of Albion Music, Inc., 1998/Warner-Chappell Music, 1998/
Remarkable, 1998/Justin Combs Music, 1998/EMI-April Music, 1998.
Revived by Puff Daddy in the film and on the soundtrack album
Godzilla (Epic Sony Soundtrax, 98).

Kenny's Dead
Words and music by Curtis Mayfield and Master P.
Big P Music, Baton Rouge, 1998/Warner-Tamerlane Music, 1998.
Revived by Master P on the album *Chef Aid: The South Park Album*
(American/Columbia, 98).

Kickin' My Heart Around
Words and music by Kenneth Donley.
Singing River Publishing Co., Inc., 1998/Unichappell Music Inc., 1998.
Best-selling record by Black Crowes on the album *By Your Side*
(American/Columbia, 98).

Kind & Generous
Words and music by Natalie Merchant.
Indian Love Bride Music, New York, 1998.
Best-selling record by Natalie Merchant from the album *Ophelia*
(Elektra, 98).

Kiss the Rain (English)
Words and music by Billie Myers, Eric Bazillian, and Desmond Child.

43

EMI-Blackwood Music Inc., 1998/EMI Songs Ltd., 1998/Polygram
International Music, 1998/WB Music, 1998/Human Boy Music, 1998.
Best-selling record by Billie Myers from the album *Growing Pains*
(Universal, 98).

Kisses Sweeter Than Wine
Words and music by Paul Campbell and Hudie Ledbetter.
Folkways Music Publishers, Inc., 1951.
Revived by Jackson Browne and Bonnie Raitt on the album *Where
Have All the Flowers Gone: The Songs of Pete Seeger* (Appleseed/
Red House, 98).

L

Lady Marmelade
Words and music by Bob Crewe and Kenny Nolan Helfman.
Stone Diamond Music, 1974/Kenny Nolan Publishing, 1974.
Revived by All Saints on the album *All Saints* (London, 98).

Lady, Your Roof Brings Me Down
Words and music by Victor Indrizzo and Scott Weiland.
Famous Music Corp., 1998.
Introduced by Scott Weiland in the film and on the soundtrack album
   Great Expectations (Atlantic, 98) and on the album *12 Bar Blues*
   (Atlantic, 98).

Landslide
Words and music by Stevie Nicks.
Welsh Witch Publishing, 1977/Sony ATV Songs, 1977.
Revived by Fleetwood Mac on the album *The Dance* (Reprise, 97).

Last Night When We Were Young
Words and music by Harold Arlen and Yip Harburg.
The Bourne Co., 1952.
Revived by David Frishberg on the album *By Himself* (Arbors Jazz, 98).

Lately
Words and music by James Baker and C. Kelly.
May King Poetry Music, 1998/Slav Tu Tu Five, 1998/Howcutt, 1998/
   Irving Music Inc., 1998.
Best-selling record by Divine from the album *Fairy Tales* (Pendulum/
   Red Ant, 98).

Laughing in the Wind (Irish)
Words and music by Van Morrison.
Caledonia Soul Music, 1973/Warner-Tamerlane Music, 1973.
Revived by Van Morrison on the album *The Philosopher's Stone*
   (Polydor, 98).

Lazarus Man
Words and music by Terry Callier.
Transmission/God is Greater, Chicago, 1998.
Introduced by Terry Callier on the album *Time Peace* (Verve Forecast, 98).

Lean on Me
Words and music by Kirk Franklin.
Lilly Mack, Inglewood, 1998/Kerrion, 1998.
Best-selling record by Kirk Franklin & The Family, featuring Mary J. Blige, Bono, R. Kelly and Crystal Lewis from the album *The Nu Nation Project* (Gospocentric/Interscope, 98). Nominated for Grammy Awards, Best R&B Song of the Year, 1998 and Best Record of the Year, 1998.

Leaving on a Jet Plane
Words and music by John Denver.
Cherry Lane Music Co., 1967.
Revived by Chantal Kreviasuk in the film and on the soundtrack album *Armageddon1* (Columbia/Sony Music Soundtrax, 98).

Let Her Go into the Darkness
Words and music by Jonathan Richman.
Rounder Music, Cambridge, 1995.
Revived by Jonathan Richman in the film and on the soundtrack album *There's Something About Mary* (Capitol, 98).

Let Me Let Go
Words and music by Steve Diamond and Dennis Morgan.
Diamond Mine, 1998/Little Shop of Morgansongs, 1998/Morgan, 1998.
Best-selling record by Faith Hill from the album *Faith* (Warner Brothers, 98).

Let's Ride
Words and music by Montel Jordan, Master P, and Silkk the Shocker.
Big P Music, Baton Rouge, 1998/Hudson Jordan, 1998/Wixen Music, 1998/Mood Swing, 1998.
Best-selling record by Montell Jordan featuring Master P & Silkk the Shocker from the album *Let's Ride* (Def Jam/Mercury, 98).

Like a Friend (English)
Words and music by Pulp and Candida Doyle.
Songs of Polygram, 1998.
Introduced by Pulp in the film and on the soundtrack album *Great Expectations* (Atlantic, 98). Also on the album *This Is Hardcore* (Island, 98).

Like You
Words and music by Kristen Hersh.

Yes Dear, 1998.
Introduced by Kristin Hersh on the album *Strange Angels* (Rykodisc, 98).

A Little Past Little Rock
Words and music by Jess Brown, Tony Lane, and Brett Jones.
Almo Music Corp., 1998/Twin Creeks, 1998/Be Le Be, 1998/Famous Music Corp., 1998.
Best-selling record by Lee Ann Womack from the album *Some Things I Know* (Decca, 98).

Little Red Rodeo
Words and music by Clint Black, Phil Vassar, and Rory Bourke.
EMI-Blackwood Music Inc., 1997/Flybridge, 1997/Sharoonie, 1997/Rory Bourke, 1997.
Best-selling record by Collin Raye from the album *The Best of Collin Raye: Direct Hits* (Epic, 98).

Livingston Saturday Night
Words and music by Jimmy Buffett.
Duchess Music Corp., 1978/Unart Music Corp., 1978.
Introduced by Jimmy Buffett in the 1975 film and on the soundtrack album *Rancho Deluxe* (Rykodisc, 98).

Lonely Won't Leave Me Alone
Words and music by Mary Danna and Jody Sweet.
Ensign Music, 1998/Joe's Cafe, 1998/MKD, 1998.
Best-selling record by Trace Adkins from the album *Big Time* (Capitol, 98).

Long Time Woman
Words and music by Les Baxter.
Quartet Music, Inc., 1971.
Revived by Pam Grier in the film *Jackie Brown* and on the soundtrack album *Jackie Brown: Music from the Miramax Motion Picture* (A Band Apart/Maverick, 98). Introduced by Grier in the 1971 film *The Big Doll House*.

A Long Way Home
Words and music by Dwight Yoakam.
Coal Dust West, 1998/Warner-Tamerlane Music, 1998.
Introduced by Dwight Yoakam on the album *A Long Way Home* (Reprise, 98).

Lookin' at Me
Words and music by Mason Betha, Chad Hugo, Sean Combs, and Pharrell Williams.
EMI-April Music, 1998/Toni Robi Music, 1998/Fat Wax, 1998/Loud and Vulgar, 1998.

Best-selling record by Mase featuring Puff Daddy from the album *Harlem World* (Bad Boy/Arista, 98).

Looking Through Your Eyes
Words and music by Carol Bayer Sager and David Foster.
Warner-Tamerlane Music, 1998.
Best-selling record by LeAnn Rimes in the film and on the soundtrack album *Quest for Camelot* (Curb/Atlantic, 98).

Love Can Move Mountains
Words and music by Diane Warren.
Realsongs, 1992.
Revived by Celine Dion with God's Property in the TV series and on the soundtrack album *Touched by an Angel* (550 Music/Sony, 98).

Love Is a Gift (Australian)
Words and music by Olivia Newton-John, Earl Rose, and Victoria Shaw.
Amadeus, New York, 1998/Zargon, Los Angeles, 1998/VLS, New York, 1998.
Introduced by Olivia Newton-John in the TV series *As the World Turns* and featured on the album *Back with a Heart*(MCA, 98).

Love Like This
Words and music by Faith Evans, Shep Crawford, Emery, Nile Rodgers, and Bernard Edwards.
Chyna Baby Music, 1998/Janice Combs Music, 1998/EMI-Blackwood Music Inc., 1998/Brother 4 Brothers, 1998/Smokin' for Lifewarner, 1998/Bernard's Other Music, 1998/Warner-Tamerlane Music, 1998/Tommy Jymi, Inc., 1998.
Best-selling record by Faith Evans from the album *Keep the Faith* (Bad Boy/Arista, 98).

Love Me
Words and music by Leslie Braithwaite, Daron Jones, Michael Keith, Quinnes Parker, Melvin Scandrick, Mason Betha, and Luther Vandross.
Rezlee, 1998/Kalinmia, 1998/Justin Combs Music, 1998/EMI-April Music, 1998/Mason Betha Music, 1998.
Best-selling record by 112 featuring Mase from the album *Room 112* (Bad Boy/Arista, 98).

Love of My Life
Words and music by Keith Stegall and Dan Hill.
Little Cayman, 1997/EMI-Blackwood Music Inc., 1997/If Dreams Had Wings, 1997.
Best-selling record by Sammy Kershaw from the album *Labor of Love* (Mercury, 98).

Love Removal Machine (English)
Words and music by Ian Astbury and William Duffy.
Chappell & Co., Inc., 1987.
Revived by Mickey Petraglia in the film and on the soundtrack album
Small Soldiers (DreamWorks, 98).

Love Shouldn't Hurt
Words and music by Steve Kipner, Jack Kugell, and Eva King.
Stephen A. Kipner Music, 1998/EMI-April Music, 1998/Foreva, 1998.
Introduced by various artists on the album *Love Shouldn't Hurt* (Qwest/
Warner Brothers, 98). Some of the artists include: Olivia Newton-
John, Michael Bolton, All-4-One, Ann Wilson, Stephen Stills, Carnie
Wilson.

Love Will Find a Way
Words and music by Jack Feldman and Tom Snow.
Wonderland Music, 1998.
Introduced by Kenny Lattimore and Heather Headley in the film and on
the soundtrack album *The Lion King II: Simba's Pride* (Walt Disney,
98).

Loverman (English)
Words and music by Nick Cave.
Windswept Pacific, 1994.
Revived by Metallica on the album *Garage Inc.* (Elektra, 98).

Lover's Will
Words and music by John Hiatt.
Careers-BMG Music, 1998.
Revived by Bonnie Raitt on the album *Fundamental* (Capitol, 98).

Loving Arms
Words and music by Tom Jans.
Almo Music Corp., 1974.
Revived by the Dixie Chicks on the album *Wide Open Spaces*
(Monument, 98).

Lullaby
Words and music by Shawn Mullins.
Shawn Mullins, 1998/Big Tooth Music Corp., 1998.
Best-selling record by Shawn Mullins from the album *Soul's Core*
(SMG/Columbia, 98).

M

Mad Sex
Words and music by Prince Rogers Nelson.
Controversy Music, 1998.
Introduced by NewPower Generation on the album *NewPower Soul* (NPG, 98).

Make Em Say Uhh!
Words and music by Master P, Silkk the Shocker, Fiend, Mia X, and Mystikal.
Burrin Avenue Music, Hollywood, 1998/Big P Music, Baton Rouge, 1998.
Best-selling record by Master P, Silkk the Shocker, Fiend, Mia X and Mystical from the album *MP da Last Don* (No Limit/Priority, 98).

Make It Hot
Words and music by Missy Elliott.
Mass Confusion Music, 1998.
Best-selling record by Nicole featuring Missy Elliott and Mocha from the album *Make It Hot* (The Gold Mine/East West, 98).

Make Use
Words and music by Robert Pollard.
Needmore Music, Minneapolis, 1998.
Introduced by Robert Pollard on the album *Waved Out* (Matador, 98).

A Man Holdin' On (to a Woman Lettin' Go)
Words and music by John Ramey, Bobby Taylor, and Gene Dobbins.
Sixteen Stars Music, 1998/Dixie Stars, 1998.
Best-selling record by Ty Herndon from the album *Big Hopes* (Epic, 98).

The Man in Me
Words and music by Bob Dylan.
Special Rider Music, 1970.

Revived by Bob Dylan in the film and on the soundtrack album *The Big Lebowsky* (Mercury, 98).

Man at the Top
Words and music by Bruce Springsteen.
Bruce Springsteen Publishing, 1984.
Revived by Bruce Springsteen on the album *Tracks* (Columbia, 98).

Midnight Radio
Words and music by Stephen Trask.
Introduced by John Cameron Mitchell in the musical *Hedwig and the Angry Inch*.

Mississippi
Words and music by Paula Cole.
Ensign Music, 1998/Hingface Music, 1998.
Introduced by Paula Cole on the album *Lilith Fair: A Celebration of Women in Music* (Arista, 98).

Mississippi
Words and music by Bob Dylan.
Special Rider Music, 1997.
Revived by Sheryl Crow on the album *The Globe Sessions* (A & M, 98).

Misty Blue
Words and music by Bob Montgomery.
Talmont Music Co., 1965.
Revived by Mary J. Blige on the album *The Tour* (MCA, 98).

Money Ain't a Thang
Words and music by Jermaine Dupri, Steve Arrington, and Shaun Carter.
EMI-April Music, 1998/So So Def Music, 1998/EMI-Blackwood Music Inc., 1998/Dunwurkin, 1998.
Best-selling record by Jermaine Dupri from the album *Life in 1472* (So So Def/Columbia, 98).

Money, Power & Respect
Words and music by Sean Jacobs, Jason Phillips, David Syles, Earl Simmons, Derek Angelettie, Ronald Lawrence, and J. Smith.
EMI-April Music, 1998/Marshall Law, 1998/Ken Meeker, 1998/EMI-Blackwood Music Inc., 1998/Aresti Arrangements, 1998/Warner-Tamerlane Music, 1998.
Best-selling record by the Lox featuring DMX & Lil' Kim from the album *Money, Power & Respect* (Bad Boy/Arista, 98).

Mose Alison Played Here
Words and music by Greg Brown.
Introduced by Greg Brown on the album *Slant 6 Mind* (Red House, 98).

Most High (English)
Words and music by Jimmy Page, Robert Plant, Charlie Jones, and
Michael Lee.
Computer Chance, 1998/Succubus Music, 1998.
Best-selling record by Page & Plant from the album *Walking into
Clarksville* (Atlantic, 98).

Mummer's Dance (Canadian)
Words and music by Loreena McKennitt.
Quinlan Road, 1998/Warner-Tamerlane Music, 1998.
Best-selling record by Loreena McKennitt from the album *The Book of
Secrets* (Warner Brothers, 98).

My All
Words and music by Mariah Carey and Walter Afanasieff.
Sony ATV Songs, 1997/Rye Songs, 1997/Sony ATV Music, 1997/Wally
World, 1997.
Best-selling record by Mariah Carey from the album *Butterfly*
(Columbia, 98).

My City Was Gone (English)
Words and music by Chrissie Hynde.
MCA Music, 1982.
Revived by Kool Keith and the Butcher Brothers in the film and on the
soundtrack album *Small Soldiers* (DreamWorks, 98).

My Father's Eyes (English)
Words and music by Eric Clapton.
E.C. Music, England, 1998/Unichappell Music Inc., 1998.
Best-selling record by Eric Clapton from the album *Pilgrim* (Reprise,
98).

My Favorite Mistake
Words and music by Sheryl Crow and Jeff Trott.
Old Crow, Los Angeles, 1998/Warner-Tamerlane Music, 1998/Wixen
Music, 1998/Trottsky Music, 1998.
Best-selling record by Sheryl Crow from the album *The Globe Sessions*
(A & M, 98).

My Heart Will Go On
Words and music by James Horner and Will Jennings.
Famous Music Corp., 1998/Irving Music Inc., 1998/Blue Sky Rider
Songs, 1998/Ensign Music, 1998/TCF Music, 1998/Fox Film Music
Corp., 1998.
Best-selling record by Celine Dion in the film and on the soundtrack

album *Titanic* and the album *Let's Talk About Love* (550 Music, 98). Won a Grammy Award for Best Song of the Year, 1998.

My Hero
Words and music by Dave Grohl, Kate Mendel, and Georg Ruthenberg. Ruthensmear, 1997/Virgin Music, 1997/MJ12 Music, 1997/Flying Earform, 1997.
Best-selling record by Foo Fighters from the album *The Colour and the Shape* (Roswell/Capitol, 97).

My Life Is Totally Boring Without You
Words and music by David Lowery, Johnny Hickman, and Bob Rupe. Biscuits and Gravy Music, 1998/Warner-Tamerlane Music, 1998.
Introduced by Cracker on the album *Gentleman's Blues* (Virgin, 98).

My Little Secret
Words and music by Jermaine Dupri, Manuel Seal, and Tamika Scott. So So Def Music, 1998/EMI-April Music, 1998/Juicy Time, 1998/Air Control Music, 1998/Slack A. D. Music, 1998/BMG Music, 1998.
Best-selling record by Xscape from the album *Traces of My Lipstick* (So So Def/Columbia, 98).

My Love Is Your Love
Words and music by Wyclef Jean and Jerry Duplessis. EMI-Blackwood Music Inc., 1998/Te Bass, 1998.
Introduced by Whitney Houston on the album *My Love Is Your Love* (Arista, 98).

My Love Will Not Let You Down
Words and music by Bruce Springsteen. Bruce Springsteen Publishing, 1982.
Revived by by Bruce Springsteen from the album *Tracks* (Columbia, 98).

My One True Friend
Words and music by Carole King, Carol Bayer Sager, and David Foster. Peer-Southern Organization, 1998/Lushmole Music, 1998/All About Me, 1998/Warner-Tamerlane Music, 1998.
Introduced by Bette Midler in the film *One True Thing*. Featured on the album *Bathhouse Bette* (Warner Brothers, 98).

My Own Peculiar Way
Words and music by Willie Nelson. Sony ATV Tree Publishing, 1966.
Revived by Willie Nelson on the album *Teatro* (Island, 98).

My Song
Words and music by Jerry Cantrell. Chris Cornell, 1998/TCF Music, 1998.

Best-selling record by Jerry Cantrell from the album *Boggy Depot* (Columbia, 98).

My Way
Words and music by Jermaine Dupri, Manuel Seal, and Usher Raymond. EMI-April Music, 1998/So So Def Music, 1998/Slack A. D. Music, 1998/UR IV Music, 1998.
Best-selling record by Usher from the album *My Way* (Arista, 98).

N

Nature Boy
Words and music by Eden Ahbez.
Golden World, Desert Hot Springs, 1948.
Revived by Victoria Williams on the album *Musings of a Creekdipper*
(Atlantic, 98).

Never Ever (English)
Words and music by Esmail Jazayer, Sean Mather, and Shaznay Lewis.
Rickety Raw, 1998/BMG Music, 1998/MCA Music, 1998.
Best-selling record by All Saints from the album *All Saints* (London/
Island, 98).

Never Going Back
Words and music by Lindsay Buckingham.
Now Sounds Music, 1977.
Revived by Matchbox 20 on the album *Legacy: A Tribute to Fleetwood
Mac* (Lava/Atlantic, 98).

Never There
Words and music by John McCrea.
EMI-Blackwood Music Inc., 1998/Stamen, 1998.
Best-selling record by Cake from the album *Prolonging the Magic*
(Capricorn/Mercury, 98).

Nice & Slow
Words and music by Usher Raymond, Harry Casey, Jermaine Dupri, and
Manuel Seal.
EMI-April Music, 1998/So So Def Music, 1998/Baba Jinde, 1998/Rock
Candy, 1998/Keel/Ko, 1998.
Best-selling record by Usher from the album *My Way* (LaFace/Arista,
97).

Ninety Nine (Flash the Message) (German)
English words and music by Joern Fahrenkrog-Peterson, Carlo Karges,
and John Forte.

EMI Songs Ltd., 1984/Additions Hate, 1984/EMI-April Music, 1984.
Best-selling record by John Forte from the album *Poly Sci* (Ruffhouse, 98).

No Easy Way (English)
Words and music by Seal (pseudonym for Sealhenry Samuel).
Perfect Songs Music, 1998.
Introduced by Seal on the album *Human Being* (Warner Brothers, 98).

No One Like You
Words and music by David Zippel and Jerry Goldsmith.
Introduced by Sarah Brightman on the album *Time to Say Goodbye* (Angel, 97). Introduced in the film *Powder*.

Nobody Does It Better
Words and music by Nate Dogg, Warren Griffin, and Johnson.
Nate Dogg Music, 1998/Almo Music Corp., 1998.
Best-selling record by Nate Dogg featuring Warren G. from the album *Gfunk Classics, Vol. 1-2* (Dogg Foundation/Epic 4000/Breakaway, 98).

Nobody's Fault but My Own
Words and music by Beck Hanson.
Cyanide Breathmint Music, 1998/BMG Songs Inc., 1998.
Introduced by Beck on the album *Mutations* (DGC, 98).

Nobody's Supposed to Be Here
Words and music by Shep Crawford and Montell Jordan.
Wixen Music, 1998/Famous Music Corp., 1998.
Best-selling record by Deborah Cox from the album *One Wish* (Arista, 98).

Nothin' But the Taillights
Words and music by Clint Black and Steve Wariner.
Blackened Music, 1997.
Best-selling record by Clint Black from the album *Nothin' But the Taillights* (RCA, 97).

Nothin' on Me
Words and music by Shawn Colvin and John Leventhal.
Lev-a-Tunes, 1997/WB Music, 1997.
Introduced by Shawn Colvin on the album *A Few Small Repairs* (Columbia, 97).

Nothing Really Matters
Words and music by Patrick Leonard and Madonna Ciccone.
WB Music, 1998/Webo Girl, 1998/No Tomato, 1998.
Introduced by Madonna on the album *Ray of Light* (Warner Brothers, 98).

Now That I Found You
Words and music by J. D. Martin, Paul Begaud, and Vanessa Corish. WB Music, 1998/Lillywilly, 1998/MCA Music, 1998/Vanessa Corish, 1998.
Best-selling record by Terri Clark from the album *How I Feel* (Mercury, 98).

O

The Oaf (My Life Is Wasted) (Canadian)
Words and music by Ian Thornley.
BGG, 1997/Sidungpoint, 1997.
Best-selling record by Big Wreck from the album *In Loving Memory Of* (Atlantic, 98).

Oh How the Years Go By (English)
Words and music by Simon Climie and Will Jennings.
Blue Sky Rider Songs, 1997/Sony ATV Songs, 1997.
Best-selling record by Vanessa Williams from the album *Next* (Mercury, 97).

Okie from Muskogee
Words and music by Merle Haggard and Roy Edward Burris.
Blue Book Music, 1969.
Revived by Leon Russell on the album *Legend in My Time: Hank Wilson, Volume III* (Ark 21, 98).

Old Man Blues
Words and music by Mose Allison.
Audre Mae Music, 1998.
Introduced by Mose Alison on the album *Gimcracks and Gewgaws* (Blue Note, 98).

On the Side of Angels
Words and music by Gary Burr and Greg House.
Red Brazos, 1997/House Notes Music, 1998/Gary Burr Music, 1998/ MCA Music, 1998.
Best-selling record by LeAnn Rimes from the album *You Light Up My Life: Inspirational Songs* (Curb, 97).

One Belief Away (Irish)
Words and music by Paul Brady, Dillon O'Brian, Bonnie Raitt, and Oliver Mutukudzi.
Warner-Tamerlane Music, 1998/Paradise American Style, 1998.

Best-selling record by Bonnie Raitt from the album *Fundamental* (Capitol, 98).

One Big Love
Words and music by Patty Griffin.
One Big Love, 1998/Chrome Dog, 1998/Polygram International Music, 1998.
Introduced by Patty Griffin on the album *Flaming Red* (A & M, 98).

One of These Days
Words and music by Kip Raines, Monte Powell, and Marcus Hummon.
Careers-BMG Music, 1997/Floyd's Dream Music, 1997/Warner-Tamerlane Music, 1997/When It Raines, 1997.
Best-selling record by Tim McGraw from the album *Everywhere* (Curb, 98).

One Week (Canadian)
Words and music by Ed Robertson.
Treat Baker Music, 1998/WB Music, 1998.
Best-selling record by Barenaked Ladies from the album *Stunt* (Reprise, 98).

Ooh La La (English)
Words and music by Ron Wood and Ronnie Lane.
WB Music, 1974.
Revived by Rod Stewart on the album *When We Were the New Boys* (Warner Brothers, 98).

Ooh My Love
Words and music by Stevie Nicks and Rich Nowels.
Welsh Witch Publishing, 1989/Streamline Moderne, 1989.
Revived by Stevie Nicks on the album *Enchanted* (Atlantic, 98).

Out of My Bones
Words and music by Gary Burr, Sharon Vaughan, and Robin Lerner.
MCA Music, 1998/Gary Burr Music, 1998/Sharondipity, 1998/Puckalesia, 1998/Nomad-Noman Music, 1998/Warner-Tamerlane Music, 1998.
Best-selling record by Randy Travis from the album *Out of My Bones* (DreamWorks, 98).

Over Your Shoulder
Words and music by Seven Mary Three.
EMI Music Publishing, 1998/7 Mary Three Music, 1998.
Best-selling record by Seven Mary Three from the album *Orange Avenue* (Atlantic, 98).

P

The Party Continues
Words and music by Jermaine Dupri, Da Brat (pseudonym for Shawntae Harris), Nathan Leftenant, Larry Blackmon, Charles Singleton, and Tomi Jenkins.
EMI-April Music, 1998/So So Def Music, 1998/Throwin' Tantrums Music, 1998/All Seeing Eye, 1998/Cameo5, 1998/WB Music, 1998/Warner-Tamerlane Music, 1998.
Best-selling record by JD featuring Da Brat from the album *Life in 1472* (So So Def/Columbia, 98).

Passionate Kisses
Words and music by Lucinda Williams.
Lucy Jones Music, 1988/Warner-Tamerlane Music, 1998/Nomad-Noman Music, 1998.
Revived by Lucinda Williams on the album *Lucinda Williams* (Mercury, 98).

Perfect
Words and music by Billy Corgan.
Cinderful Music, 1998/Chrysalis Music Group, 1998.
Best-selling record by Smashing Pumpkins from the album *Ava Adore* (Virgin, 98).

A Perfect Day Elise (English)
Words and music by Polly Jean Harvey.
EMI-Blackwood Music Inc., 1998.
Best-selling record by PJ Harvey from the album *Is This Desire* (Island, 98).

Perfect Love
Words and music by Sunny Russ and Stephony Smith.
Starstruck Angel Music, 1998/Missoula, 1998/EMI-Blackwood Music Inc., 1998/Single's Only, 1998.
Best-selling record by Trisha Yearwood from the album *(Songbook) A Collection of Hits* (MCA Nashville, 98).

Playing with Jack
Words and music by Peter Case.
Trumpet Blast Music, 1998.
Introduced by The Plimsouls on the album *Kool Trash* (Musidisc, 98).

Playing Your Song
Words and music by Eric Erlandson, Courtney Love, and Melissa Auf Der Mar.
Mother May I, Sherman Oaks, 1998.
Introduced by Hole on the album *Celebrity Skin* (DGC, 98).

Polyester Bride
Words and music by Liz Phair.
Sony ATV Songs, 1998.
Introduced by Liz Phair on the album *whitechocolatespaceegg* (Matador, 98).

Power of Goodbye
Words and music by Madonna Ciccone and Rich Nowels.
Webo Girl, 1998/EMI-April Music, 1998/Streamline Moderne, 1998/WB Music, 1998.
Introduced by Madonna on the album *Ray of Light* (Maverick/Warner Brothers, 98). Also featured on the TV series *Felicity*.

The Prayer (Canadian)
Words and music by David Foster and Carole Bayer Sager.
EMI-Blackwood Music Inc., 1998.
Introduced by Celine Dion in the film *Quest for Camelot* (Curb/Warner Sunset/Atlantic, 98). Performed in the film by Andrea Bocelli.
Nominated for an Academy Award, Best Song of the Year, 1998.

Premonition
Words and music by John Fogerty.
Cody River Music, Sherman Oaks, 1998.
Best-selling record by John Fogerty from the album *Premonition* (Reprise, 98).

Pretty Fly (For a White Guy)
Words and music by Offspring.
Underachiever Music, Calabasas, 1998/Wixen Music, 1998.
Best-selling record by the Offspring from the album *Americana* (Epic, 98).

Psycho Circus
Words and music by Paul Stanley and Curt Cuomo.
Ri Ho, 1998/Hook Mo, 1998/Songs of Polygram, 1998.
Best-selling record by Kiss from the album *Psycho Circus* (Mercury, 98).

Psycho Man (English)
Words and music by Ozzy Osbourne and Tony Iommi.
Black Lava, Woodland Hills, 1998/Vallallen, 1998.
Best-selling record by Black Sabbath from the album *Reunion* (Epic, 98).

Pulse
Words and music by Ani DiFranco.
Righteous Babe Music, Buffalo, 1998.
Introduced by Ani DiFranco on the album *Little Plastic Castle* (Righteous Babe, 98).

Push It
Words and music by Duke Erickson, Shirley Manson, Steve Marker, and Butch Vig.
Irving Music Inc., 1998/Vibe Crusher Music, 1998.
Best-selling record by Garbage from the album *Garbage Version 2.0* (Almo Sounds/Interscope, 98).

R

Raindrops Keep Falling on My Head
Words and music by Burt Bacharach and Hal David.
WB Music, 1969/Casa David, 1969/Twentieth Century-Fox Music Corp., 1998.
Revived by Shonen Knife on the album *What the World Needs Now: Big Deal Recording Artists Perform the Songs of Burt Bacharach* (Big Deal, 98).

Rapid City, South Dakota
Words and music by Richard Friedman.
Ensign Music, 1975.
Revived by Dwight Yoakam on the album *Pearls in the Snow: The Songs of Kinky Friedman* (Kinkajou, 98).

Raspberry Swirl
Words and music by Tori Amos.
Sword and Stone Music, 1998.
Introduced by Tori Amos on the album *From the Choirgirl Hotel* (Atlantic, 98).

Ray of Light (American-English)
Words and music by Madonna Ciccone, William Orbit, Dave Curtis, Clive Muldoon, and Christine Leach.
WB Music, 1998/Webo Girl, 1998/Rondor Music Inc., 1998/Almo Music Corp., 1998.
Best-selling record by Madonna from the album *Ray of Light* (Warner Brothers, 98). Nominated for a Grammy Award, Best Record of the Year, 1998.

Real World
Words and music by Rob Thomas.
EMI-Blackwood Music Inc., 1997/Bidnis Inc Music, 1997.
Best-selling record by Matchbox 20 from the album *Yourself or Someone Like You* (Lava/Atlantic, 97).

Reconsider Me
Words and music by Warren Zevon.
Zevon Music Inc., 1987.
Revived by Stevie Nicks on the album *Enchanted* (Modern/Atlantic, 98).

Reflection
Words and music by Matthew Wilder and David Zippel.
Walt Disney Music, 1998.
Introduced by Christina Aguilera in the film and on the soundtrack
album *Mulan* (Walt Disney, 98).

Replenished
Words and music by Vic Chesnutt.
Ghetto Bells Music, 1998.
Best-selling record by Vic Chesnutt from the album *The Salesman and
Bernadette* (Capricorn, 98).

Reunion Hill
Words and music by Richard Shindell.
Richard Shindell Music, Chesterfield, 1998.
Introduced by Richard Shindell on the album *Reunion Hill* (Shanachie,
97).

Right on the Money
Words and music by Clint Black and Phil Vassar.
EMI-Blackwood Music Inc., 1998/Flybridge, 1998/EMI-April Music,
1998/Phil Vassar, 1998.
Best-selling record by Alan Jackson from the album *High Mileage*
(Arista Nashville, 98).

Right in Time
Words and music by Lucinda Williams.
Lucy Jones Music, 1998/Warner-Tamerlane Music, 1998/Nomad-Noman
Music, 1998.
Introduced by Lucinda Williams on the album *Car Wheels on a Gravel
Road* (Mercury, 98).

Rock-a-Hula Baby
Words and music by Dolores Fuller, Ben Weiss, and Fred Wise.
Bienstock Publishing Co., 1962/Chappell & Co., Inc., 1962/Erika, 1962.
Revived by Junior Brown on the album *Long Walk Back* (Curb, 98).

Rock Steady
Words and music by Aretha Franklin.
Springtime Music Inc., 1972.
Revived by Dawn Robinson in the film and on the soundtrack album
Dr. Doolittle (Atlantic, 97).

The Rockafella Skank (English)
Words and music by Fatboy Slim (pseudonym for Norman Cook), John Barry, and Terry Winford.
Polygram Music Publishing Inc., 1998.
Best-selling record by Fatboy Slim from the album *MTV's Amp2* (Skint/ Astralwerks, 98). Also included on the album *You've Come a Long Way Baby* (Astralwerks, 98).

Romeo and Juliet
Words and music by Lamar Johnson, Victor Merritt, Angela Winbush, Rene Moore, William Werner, and Gerald Baillergeau.
Virgin Music, 1998/Rene Moore, 1998/A La Mode Music, 1998/Les Editions Musicale, 1998/Micon Publishing, 1998.
Best-selling record by Sylk E. Fyne featuring Chill from the album *Raw Sylk* (Grand Jury/RCA, 98).

Rosa Parks
Words and music by Andre Benjamin and Antwan Patton.
Gnat Booty Music, 1998/Chrysalis Music Group, 1998.
Introduced by OutKast on the album *Aquemini* (LaFace/Arista, 98).

A Rose Is Still a Rose
Words and music by Lauryn Hill, Edie Brickell, and Kenny Withrow.
Sony ATV Music, 1998/Obverse Creation Music, 1998/MCA Music, 1998/Enlightened Kitty, 1998/Strange Mind Productions, 1998/Edie Brickell Songs, 1998/Withrow Publishing, 1998/Geffen Music, 1998.
Best-selling record by Aretha Franklin from the album *A Rose Is Still a Rose* (Arista, 98). Nominated for a Grammy Award, Best R&B Song of the Year, 1998.

Roulette
Words and music by Bruce Springsteen.
Bruce Springsteen Publishing, 1979.
Revived by by Bruce Springsteen on the album *Tracks* (Columbia, 98).

Round About Way
Words and music by Steven Dean and Willard Nance.
O-Tex Music, 1998/Tom Collins Music Corp., 1998/Still Working for the Man Music, 1998.
Best-selling record by George Strait from the album *One Step at a Time* (MCA Nashville, 98).

S

Sailing Down This Golden River
Words and music by Pete Seeger.
Melody Trails Inc., 1971.
Revived by Greg Brown on the album *Where Have All the Flowers Gone: The Songs of Pete Seeger* (Appleseed/Red House, 98).

Saint Joe on the School Bus
Words and music by John Wozniak.
WB Music, 1998.
Best-selling record by Marcy Playground from the album *Marcy Playground* (Capitol, 98).

Save Tonight
Words and music by Eagle Eye Cherry.
Warner-Tamerlane Music, 1998.
Best-selling record by Eagle Eye Cherry from the album *Desireless* (Work, 98).

Save Yourself
Words and music by Andrew Kubiszewski, Christopher Hall, Walter Flakus, James Sellers, and Marcus Eliopulus.
Virgin Music, 1998.
Best-selling record by Stabbing Westward from the album *Darkest Days* (Columbia, 98).

Say It
Words and music by Raymond Basora, Steve Morales, and Gerard McKetney.
Stingray Sounds, 1998/Jelly's Jams L.L.C. Music, 1998/Gem, 1998/Million Dollar Steve, 1998/Jumping Bean Music, 1998.
Best-selling record by Voices of Theory from the album *Voices of Theory* (H.O. LA/Red Ant, 98).

Schooldays
Words and music by Loudon Wainwright.

Snowden Music, 1970.
Revived by Loudon Wainwright on the album *The McGarrigle Hour* (Hannibal/Rykodisc, 98).

Scooter Boys
Words and music by Amy Ray and Emily Saliers.
Virgin Music, 1998/Godhap Music, 1998.
Revived by The Indigo Girls from the album *Lilith Fair: A Celebration of Women in Music* (Arista, 98).

Searchin' My Soul
Words and music by Vonda Shepherd.
TCF Music, 1997.
Best-selling record by Vonda Shepherd in the TV series *Ally McBeal* and soundtrack album *Songs from Ally McBeal* (550/Epic, 98).

Second Round K.O.
Words and music by Germaine Williams, Wyclef Jean, Jerry Wonder, Gordon Chambers, Thom Bell, Kenny Gamble, and Jerry Duplessis.
EMI-April Music, 1998/EMI-Blackwood Music Inc., 1998/Downright Dizzy, 1998/Darron Williams, 1998/Amokshasong, 1998.
Best-selling record by Canibus from the album *Can-I-Bus* (Universal, 98).

Secret Heart (English)
Words and music by Ron Sexsmith.
Music Corp. of America, 1995.
Revived by by Rod Stewart on the album *When We Were the New Boys* (Warner Brothers, 98).

Secrets and Lies
Words and music by Jonatha Brooke.
Dog Dream, 1997.
Best-selling record by Jonatha Brooke on the album *10 Cent Wings* (Refuge/MCA, 98).

Seymour Stein
English words and music by Steve Jackson.
Introduced by Belle and Sebastian on the album *The Boy with the Arab Strap* (Matador, 98).

Shadowland
Words and music by Hans Zimmer, Lebo M., and Mark Mancino.
Walt Disney Music, 1997/Wonderland Music, 1997.
Introduced by the original cast of the Lion King in the musical and cast album *The Lion King* (Walt Disney, 97).

She Used to Say That to Me
Words and music by Jim Lauderdale and John Scott Sherrill.

Mighty Nice Music, 1995/New Wolf Music, 1995/Sony ATV Tree
Publishing, 1998.
Introduced by Jim Lauderdale on the album *Whisper* (BNA, 98).

Shelf in My Room
Words and music by Travis Meeks.
Scrogrow Music, 1998/Warner-Tamerlane Music, 1998.
Best-selling record by Days of the New from the album *Days of the
New* (Outpost/Geffen, 98).

Shimmer
Words and music by Carl Bell.
Songs of Polygram, 1998/Pener Pig, 1998.
Best-selling record by Fuel from the album *Sunburn* (550/Epic, 98).

Shining in the Light (English)
Words and music by Jimmy Page, Robert Plant, Charlie Jones, and
Michael Lee.
WB Music, 1998.
Best-selling record by Page & Plant from the album *Walking into
Clarksville* (Atlantic, 98).

The Shoes You're Wearing
Words and music by Clint Black and Hayden Nicholas.
Blackened Music, 1997.
Best-selling record by Clint Black from the album *Nothin' But the
Taillights* (RCA, 97).

Siren
Words and music by Tori Amos and Patrick Doyle.
Sword and Stone Music, 1997.
Introduced by Tori Amos in the film and on the soundtrack album *Great
Expectations* (Atlantic, 98).

Sisters
Words and music by Irving Berlin.
Williamson Music, 1954.
Revived by Emily Skinner and Alice Ripley on the album *Duets* (Varese
Sarabande, 98).

Skin
Words and music by Madonna Ciccone and Patrick Leonard.
WB Music, 1998/No Tomato, 1998.
Introduced by Madonna on the album *Ray of Light* (Warner Brothers,
98).

Slide
Words and music by John Rzeznick.
Corner of Clark and Kent, 1998/Virgin Music, 1998.

73

Best-selling record by the Goo Goo Dolls from the album *Dizzy Up the Girl* (Warner Brothers, 98).

So Many People
Words and music by Stephen Sondheim.
Chappell & Co., Inc., 1954.
Revived by the Bridewell Theatre Company in the musical and on the cast album *Saturday Night* (RCA, 98).

Socks, Drugs and Rock and Roll (Japanese)
English words and music by Sugar Yoshinaga and Yumiko Ohno.
Introduced by Buffalo Daughter on the album *New Rock* (Grand Royal, 97).

A Soft Place to Fall
Words and music by Allison Moorer and Gwil Owen.
Longitude Music, 1998/Louise Red, 1998/Turgid Tunes, 1998/Bug Music, 1998.
Introduced by Allison Moorer in the film and on the soundtrack album *The Horse Whisperer* (MCA Nashville, 98). Also featured on the album *Alabama Song* (MCA Nashville, 98). Nominated for an Academy Award, Best Song of the Year, 1998.

Somehow, Somewhere, Someway
Words and music by Kenny Wayne Shepherd and Danny Tate.
Music Corp. of America, 1998/Only Hit Music, 1998.
Best-selling record by Kenny Wayne Shepherd from the album *Trouble Is* (Revolution, 98).

Someone You Used to Know
Words and music by Roy Lee and Tim Johnson.
Melanie Howard, 1998/Big Giant Music, 1998.
Best-selling record by Collin Raye from the album *The Walls Came Down* (Epic, 98).

Song of Being a Child (Irish)
Words and music by Peter Handke and Van Morrison.
Songs of Polygram, 1998.
Introduced by Van Morrison on the album *The Philosopher's Stone* (Polydor, 98).

Song for the Dumped
Words and music by Ben Folds and Daron Jessee.
Sony ATV Songs, 1997/Hair Sucker, 1997.
Introduced by Ben Folds Five on the album *Whatever and Ever Amen* (550 Music, 97).

Songbird (English)
Words and music by Christine McVie.

Fleetwood Mac Music Ltd., 1977.
Revived by Duncan Sheik on the album *Legacy: A Tribute to Fleetwood Mac* (Lava/Atlantic, 98).

Soulful Old Man Sunshine
Words and music by Brian Wilson, Richard Henn, and Donald Ralke.
Insongnia, Malibu, 1969/Dee Cam Publishing, Santa Rosa, 1969/Bri-Murn Music, 1969.
Revived by the Beach Boys on the album *Endless Harmony Soundtrack* (Capitol, 98).

South American
Words and music by Brian Wilson, Jimmy Buffett, and Joseph Thomas.
Coral Reefer Music, 1998/New Executive Music, 1998/On the Fox, 1998.
Introduced by Brian Wilson on the album *Imagination* (Giant, 98).

Space Lord
Words and music by Dave Wyndorf.
Songs of Polygram, 1998/Bull God, 1998.
Best-selling record by Monster Magnet from the album *Powertrip* (A & M, 98).

Stand by Your Man
Words and music by Billy Sherrill and Tammy Wynette.
EMI Music Publishing, 1968/Al Gallico Music Corp., 1968.
Revived by Elton John on the album *Tammy Wynette: Remembered* (Asylum, 98). Also Revived by Tammy Wynette (Epic, 98).

Stay in Touch
Words and music by Joni Mitchell.
Crazy Crow Music, 1998/Sony ATV Songs, 1998.
Introduced by Joni Mitchell on the album *Taming the Tiger* (Reprise, 98).

Still Crazy After All These Years
Words and music by Paul Simon.
Paul Simon Music, 1975.
Revived by New York Voices on the album *Sing the Songs of Paul Simon* (RCA, 98).

Still a G Thang
Words and music by Calvin Broadus and Cecil Womack.
My Own Chit, 1998/Cina, 1998.
Best-selling record by Snoop Dogg from the album *Da Game Is to Be Sold, Not to Be Told* (No Limit/Priority, 98).

Still I Long for Your Kiss
Words and music by Lucinda Williams.

Lucy Jones Music, 1997/Warner-Tamerlane Music, 1997/Nomad-Noman Music, 1997.
Introduced by Lucinda Williams in the film and on the soundtrack album *The Horse Whisperer* (MCA Nashville, 98). Revived on the album *Car Wheels on a Gravel Road* (Mercury, 98).

Still Not a Player
Words and music by Brenda Russell, Jerome Foster, Michelle Williams, Rodney Jerkins, Japhe Tejeda, Joe Thomas, and Jolyon Skinner.
Let Me Show You, 1998/Joe Cartegena, 1998/Jelly's Jams L.L.C. Music, 1998/Sounds of Da Red Drum, 1998/Almo Music Corp., 1998/Rutland Road, 1998/Foray, 1998/1972 Music, 1998.
Best-selling record by Big Punisher featuring Joe from the album *Capital Punishment* (Loud/RCA, 98).

Stop (English)
Words and music by Spice Girls, words and music by Wayne Watkins and Paul Wilson.
Full Keel Music, 1998/Windswept Pacific, 1998/45 Music, 1998/BMG Music, 1998.
Best-selling record by the Spice Girls from the album *Spice World* (Virgin, 97).

Stormy Weather
Words and music by Harold Arlen, Ted Koehler, and Fred Ahlert.
Sa, Smithtown, 1933.
Revived by Royal Crown Revue on the album *The Contender* (Warner Brothers, 98).

Streets of Baltimore
Words and music by Harlan Howard and Tompall Glaser.
Ensign Music, 1966.
Revived by Nanci Griffith on the album *Other Voices, Too (A Trip Back to Bountiful)* (Elektra, 98).

Strychnine
Words and music by Gerald Roglie.
Valet, Seattle, 1998.
Revived by the Sonics on the album *Nuggets: Original Artyfacts from the First Psychedelic Era 1965-1968* (Rhino, 98).

Stupid Blues
Words and music by Junior Brown.
Jameison Brown Music, 1998/Mike Curb Productions, 1998.
Introduced by Junior Brown on the album *Long Walk Back* (Curb, 98).

Sugar Sugar
Words and music by Jeff Barry and Andy Kim.

EMI-Blackwood Music Inc., 1969.
Revived by the Archies (32 Records, 98).

Sunflower Cat (Some Dour Cat) (Down with That)
Words and music by Bruce Hornsby.
Basically Zappo Music, 1998/Warner-Chappell Music, 1998.
Introduced by Bruce Hornsby on the album *Spirit Trail* (RCA, 98).

Sunshower
Words and music by Jerry Cantrell.
Chris Cornell, 1998/TCF Music, 1998.
Best-selling record by Jerry Cantrell in the film and on the soundtrack
    album *Great Expectations* (Atlantic, 97). Also on the album *Boggy
    Depot* (Columbia, 98).

Sweet Surrender (Canadian)
Words and music by Sarah McLachlan and Pierre Marchand.
Sony ATV Music, 1997/Studio Nomado Music, 1997.
Best-selling record by Sarah McLachlan on the album *Surfacing* (Arista,
    97).

Sweetest Thing (Irish)
Words and music by Adam Clayton, Laurence Mullen, Paul Hewson,
    and Dave Evans.
Polygram International Music, 1987.
Revived by U2 on the album *U2: Greatest Hits* (Island, 98).

Sweetheart
Words and music by Rainy Davis and Pete Warner.
MCA Music Co. Inc. Publishing, 1985.
Revived by JD and Mariah on the album *Life in 1472* (So So Def/
    Columbia, 98).

Swing My Way
Words and music by Michael Johnson, Javalyn Hall, Carlton Mahone,
    and Chris Briages.
Horrible, 1997.
Best-selling record by K.P & Envyi from the album *Rhythm & Quad
    166, Vol. 1* (EastWest, 98).

T

Take on Me (Norwegian)
English words and music by Pal Weaktaar, Mags Furuholem, and Marten Harket.
Sony ATV Music, 1985.
Revived by Reel Big Fish in the film and on the soundtrack album *Baseketball* (Mojo, 98).

Taking Everything
Words and music by Bob Mould.
Granary Music, 1998.
Introduced by Bob Mould on the album *The Last Dog and Pony Show* (Rykodisc, 98).

(Talk to Me of) Mendocino (Canadian)
Words and music by Kate McGarrigle.
Garden Court Music Co., 1975.
Revived by McGarrigles on the album *The McGarrigle Hour* (Hannibal/ Rykodisc, 98).

Teach Me How to Love You
Words and music by Jeffrey Stock and Susan Birkenhead.
Chappell & Co., Inc., 1997.
Revived by Betty Buckley, F. Murray Abraham, and Susan Egan in the cast album *Triumph of Love* (Jay, 98).

Tear
Words and music by Billy Corgan.
Cinderful Music, 1998/Chrysalis Music Group, 1998.
Introduced by Smashing Pumpkins on the album *Ava Adore* (Virgin, 98).

Texas Size Heartache
Words and music by Zack Turner and William Wilson.
Sony ATV Tree Publishing, 1998/Sony ATV Cross Keys Publishing Co. Inc., 1998.

Best-selling record by Joe Diffie from the album *Joe Diffie: Greatest Hits* (Epic, 98).

Thank U
Words and music by Alanis Morrisette and Glen Ballard.
Norick Music, Leona, 1998/MCA Music, 1998/Aerostation Corp., 1998.
Best-selling record by Alanis Morrisette from the album *Supposed Former Infatuation Junkie* (Maverick/Reprise, 98).

That I Would Be Good
Words and music by Alanis Morrisette and Glen Ballard.
Norick Music, Leona, 1998/MCA Music, 1998/Aerostation Corp., 1998.
Introduced by Alanis Morrisette on the album *Supposed Former Infatuation Junkie* (Maverick/Reprise, 98).

That'll Do
Words and music by Randy Newman.
Randy Newman Music, 1998/MCA Music, 1998.
Introduced by Peter Gabriel featuring Paddy Maloney and the Black Dyke Mills Band in the film and on the soundtrack album *Babe-Pig in the City* (Geffen, 98). Nominated for an Academy Award, Best Song of the Year, 1998.

That's Why I'm Here
Words and music by Shaye Smith and Mark Alan Springer.
EMI-Blackwood Music Inc., 1997/Mark Alan Springer Music, 1997.
Best-selling record by Kenny Chesney from the album *I Will Stand* (BNA, 97).

Then What
Words and music by Randy Sharp and John Vezner.
Windswept Pacific, 1998/Warner-Tamerlane Music, 1998/Minnesota Man, 1998/Areles, 1998/Wedgewood Avenue Music, 1998.
Best-selling record by Clay Walker from the album *Clay Walker: Greatest Hits* (Giant/Reprise, 98).

There Goes My Baby
Words and music by Annie Roboff and Arnie Roman.
Almo Music Corp., 1998/Anwa Music, 1998/Romanesque, 1998/Anotation, 1998/WB Music, 1998.
Best-selling record by Trisha Yearwood from the album *Where Your Road Leads* (MCA Nashville, 98).

There's Your Trouble
Words and music by Tia Sillers and Mark Selby.
Tom Collins Music Corp., 1998/Magnasong, 1998.
Best-selling record by the Dixie Chicks from the album *Wide Open Spaces* (Monument, 98).

They Don't Know
Words and music by Jonathan Buck, Bob Robinson, and Tim Kelley.
Cherry Lane Music Co., 1998/Yab Yum, 1998/Vibzelect, 1998/Time for Flytes Music, 1998.
Best-selling record by Jon B. from the album *Cool Relax* (Yab Yum/550 Music, 98).

Thinkin' Bout It
Words and music by Darrell Allamby, Lincoln Browder, and Antionette Robertson.
2000 Watts Music, Newark, 1998/WB Music, 1998/Toni Robi Music, 1998/Zomba Music, 1998/Divided, 1998.
Best-selling record by Gerald Levert from the album *Love & Consequences* (EastWest, 98).

32 Flavors
Words and music by Ani DiFranco.
Righteous Babe Music, Buffalo, 1995.
Revived by Alana Davis on the album *Blame It on Me* (Elektra, 98).

This Is Hardcore (English)
Words and music by Jarvis Cocker, Nick Banks, Candida Doyle, Steve Mackey, Mark Webber, and Peter Thomas.
Songs of Polygram, 1998/Ring Musik, 1998.
Introduced by Pulp on the album *This Is Hardcore* (Island, 98).

This Kiss
Words and music by Robin Lerner, Annie Roboff, and Beth Neilsen Chapman.
Puckalesia, 1998/Nomad-Noman Music, 1998/Warner-Tamerlane Music, 1998/Almo Music Corp., 1998/BNC, 1998/Anwa Music, 1998.
Best-selling record by Faith Hill from the album *Faith* (Warner Brothers, 98). Introduced by Faith Hill in the film and on the soundtrack album *Practical Magic* (Warner Sunset/Atlantic, 97). Nominated for a Grammy Award, Best Country Song of the Year, 1998.

Thundercrack
Words and music by Bruce Springsteen.
Bruce Springsteen Publishing, 1972.
Revived by by Bruce Springsteen on the album *Tracks* (Columbia, 98).

Tiger Woods
Words and music by Dan Bern.
Kababa Music, Los Angeles, 1998.
Introduced by Dan Bern on the album *Fifty Eggs* (Work, 98).

Time After Time
Words and music by Cyndi Lauper and Rob Hyman.

Sony ATV Songs, 1984/Rella Music Corp., 1984/Dub Notes, 1984/WB
Music, 1984.
Revived by Inoj on the album *Bass All-Stars* (So So Def/Columbia, 98).

To Get Me to You
Words and music by Diane Warren.
Diane Warren Trust, 1998/Realsongs, 1998.
Introduced by Lila McCann in the film and on the soundtrack album
Hope Floats (Capitol, 98).

To Have You Back Again
Words and music by Annie Roboff and Arnie Roman.
Almo Music Corp., 1997/WB Music, 1997.
Best-selling record by Patty Loveless from the album *Long Stretch of
Lonesome* (Epic, 98).

To Love You More (Canadian)
Words and music by David Foster, Junior Miles, and Edgar Bronfman.
MCA Music, 1998/Peer-Southern Organization, 1998.
Best-selling record by Celine Dion from the album *Let's Talk About
Love* (550/Epic, 98).

To Make You Feel My Love
Words and music by Bob Dylan.
Special Rider Music, 1998.
Revived by Garth Brooks and Trisha Yearwood in the film and on the
soundtrack album *Hope Floats* (Capitol, 98). Nominated for a
Grammy Award, Best Country Song of the Year, 1998.

To Zion
Words and music by Lauryn Hill, Norman Gimble, and Charles Fox.
Fox-Gimbel Productions, 1998/Rodali, 1998/Sony ATV Music, 1998.
Introduced by Lauryn Hill on the album *The Miseducation of Lauryn
Hill* (Ruffhouse/Columbia, 98).

Too Close
Words and music by Keir Gist, Darren Lighty, Robert Huggar, Raphael
Brown, Robert Ford, Denzil Miller, James Moore, and Kurt Walker.
WB Music, 1998/Neutral Gray Music, 1998/Pure Love, 1998/Naughty,
1998.
Best-selling record by Next from the album *Rated Next* (Arista, 97).

Too Good to Be True
Words and music by Gene Pistilli and Michael Peterson.
Warner-Tamerlane Music, 1998/Milene Music Inc., 1998.
Best-selling record by Michael Peterson from the album *Michael
Peterson* (Reprise, 98).

Too Much (English)
Words and music by Spice Girls, Wayne Watkins, and Paul Wilson.
BMG Songs Inc., 1998/Windswept, 1998.
Best-selling record by the Spice Girls from the album *Spice World* (Virgin, 97).

Torn (Australian)
Words and music by Phil Thornally, Scott Cutler, and Anne Preven.
BMG Songs Inc., 1995/Colgems-EMI Music, 1995/Songs of Polygram, 1995/Weetie Pie, 1995.
Best-selling record by Natalie Imbruglia from the album *Left of the Middle* (RCA, 98).

Touch It
Words and music by Jack Knight, Albert Charles, Tim Stahl, and Monifah Guld.
Andy Heath, 1998/Music Impossible, 1998/Polygram International Music, 1998.
Best-selling record by Monifah from the album *Mo'hogany* (Uptown/Universal, 98).

Traveler's Lantern
Words and music by Dwight Yoakam.
Coal Dust West, 1998/Warner-Tamerlane Music, 1998.
Introduced by Dwight Yoakam on the album *A Long Way Home* (Reprise, 98).

Trippin'
Words and music by Missy Elliott, Daryl Pearson, and Mike Mosley.
Wacissa River Music, Nashville, 1998/Mass Confusion Music, 1998/WB Music, 1998/Virginia Beach Music, 1998.
Best-selling record by Total featuring Missy Elliott from the album *Kima, Keisha & Pam* (Bad Boy/Arista, 98).

True
Words and music by Marv Green and Jeff Stevens.
Warner-Tamerlane Music, 1998/Jeff Stevens Music, 1998/Felder Pomus, 1998.
Best-selling record by George Strait from the album *One Step at a Time* (MCA Nashville, 98).

True Colors
Words and music by Billy Steinberg and Tom Kelly.
Sony ATV Music, 1984.
Revived by Phil Collins on the album *Phil Collins...Hits* (Atlantic, 98).

True to Your Heart
Words and music by Matthew Wilder and David Zippel.
Walt Disney Music, 1998.

Introduced by 98 Degrees and Stevie Wonder in the film and on the soundtrack album *Mulan* (Walt Disney, 98).

Truly, Truly
Words and music by Grant Lee Phillips.
Storm Hymnal Music, Los Angeles, 1998/Warner-Tamerlane Music, 1998.
Best-selling record by Grant Lee Buffalo from the album *Jubilee* (Slash/Warner Brothers, 98).

Turn It Up (Remix)
Words and music by Trevor Smith and Al Green.
Irving Music Inc., 1998/Warner-Tamerlane Music, 1998/T'Ziah's Music, 1998.
Best-selling record by Busta Rhymes from the album *When Disaster Strikes* (Elektra, 98).

Turn the Page
Words and music by Bob Seger.
Hideout Records/Distributing Co., 1984.
Revived by Metallica on the album *Garage Inc.* (Elektra, 98).

26 Cents (Canadian)
Words and music by Steve Wilkinson and William Wallace.
Golden Phoenix, 1998/Kiayasong, 1998.
Best-selling record by The Wilkinsons from the album *Nothing But Love* (Giant/Reprise, 98).

Two Pina Coladas
Words and music by Shawn Camp, Benita Hill, and Sandy Mason.
Foreshadow Songs, Inc., 1998/CMI America, 1998/Shawn Camp, 1998/Good, 1998.
Best-selling record by Garth Brooks from the album *Sevens* (Capitol Nashville, 98).

Waltz #2 (XO)
Words and music by Elliott Smith.
Spent Bullets Music, 1998/Careers-BMG Music, 1998.
Introduced by Elliott Smith on the album *XO* (DreamWorks, 98).

U

U Like Pina Coladas
Words and music by Rupert Holmes and Charles Trahan.
Holmes Line of Music, 1998/WB Music, 1998.
Best-selling record by the Bass All-Stars from the album *And Then There Was Bass* (LaFace/Arista, 98).

Umbrella Man
Words and music by Mark Michaels.
Sheek Louchion Music, 1998.
Revived by Umbrella Man (Bong, 98).

Unbound
Words and music by Robbie Robertson and Tim Gordine.
WB Music, 1998.
Introduced by Robbie Robertson on the album *Contact from the Underworld of Red Boy* (Capitol, 98).

The Unforgiven II
Words and music by Kirk Hammett, James Hetfield, and Lars Ulrich.
Creeping Death Music, 1998.
Best-selling record by Metallica from the album *Reload* (Elektra, 98).

Uninvited
Words and music by Alanis Morrisette.
MCA Music, 1998.
Introduced by Alanis Morrisette in the film and on the soundtrack album *City of Angels* (Warner Sunset/Reprise, 98). Won a Grammy Award for Best Song of the Year, 1998.

The Unwelcome Guest (English)
Words and music by Billy Bragg and Woody Guthrie.
Ludlow Music Inc., 1998.
Introduced by Billy Bragg and Wilco on the album *Mermaid Avenue* (Elektra, 98).

V

Victory
Words and music by Christopher Wallace, Jason Phillips, Sean Combs, Steven Jordan, and William Conti.
EMI-April Music, 1997/Aruba, 1997/Essex Music International, 1997.
Best-selling record by Puff Daddy & the Family featuring the Notorious B.I.G. and Busta Rhymes from the album *No Way Out* (Bad Boy/Arista, 97).

Video Killed the Radio Star (English)
Words and music by Geoffrey Downes, Trevor Horn, and Bruce Wooley.
Carbert Music Inc., 1979.
Revived by The Presidents of the United States in the film and on the soundtrack album *The Wedding Singer* (Maverick/Warner Brothers, 98).

Viva Las Vegas
Words and music by Doc Pomus and Mort Shuman.
Felder Pomus, 1964/Sharoonie, 1964/Pomus, 1964/Mort Shuman, 1998.
Revived by the Dead Kennedys in the film and on the soundtrack album *Fear and Loathing in Las Vegas* (Geffen, 98).

W

Walk Away Renee
Words and music by Michael Lookofsky, Bob Calilli, and Tony
Sansone.
Alley Music, 1966/Trio Music Co., Inc., 1966.
Revived by Vonda Shepherd in the TV show Ally McBeal and on the
soundtrack album *Songs from Ally McBeal* (550 Music, 98).

Walk on By
Words and music by Burt Bacharach and Hal David.
Casa David, 1964/WB Music, 1964.
Revived by Cockeyed Ghost on the album *What the World Needs Now:
Big Deal Recording Artists Perform the Songs of Burt Bacharach*
(Big Deal, 98).

Walt Whitman's Niece (English)
Words and music by Billy Bragg and Woody Guthrie.
Woody Guthrie Publications, 1998.
Introduced by Billy Bragg and Wilco on the album *Mermaid Avenue*
(Elektra, 98).

War
Words and music by Norman Whitfield and Barrett Strong.
Stone Agate Music, 1970.
Revived by Henry Rollins and Bone Thugs-N-Harmony in the film and
on the soundtrack album *Small Soldiers* (DreamWorks, 98).

The Way
Words and music by Tony Scalzo.
EMI-April Music, 1998.
Best-selling record by Fastball from the album *All the Pain That Money
Can Buy* (Hollywood, 98).

Way Over Yonder in the Minor Key (English)
Words and music by Billy Bragg and Woody Guthrie.
Woody Guthrie Publications, 1998.

Introduced by Billy Bragg and Natalie Merchant on the album *Mermaid Avenue* (Elektra, 98).

We Be Clubbin'
Words and music by Ice Cube (pseudonym for O'Shea Jackson) and Richard Cousin.
Sony ATV Music, 1998/Music Everyone Craves, 1998/WB Music, 1998.
Introduced by Ice Cube in the film *The Players Club* and on the soundtrack album *The Players Club: Music from and Inspired by the Motion Picture* (Heavyweight Records/A & M, 98).

We Had It All
Words and music by Donnie Fritts and Troy Seals.
Danor Music Inc., 1973.
Revived by Donnie Fritts on the album *Everybody's Got a Song* (Oh Boy, 98).

We Really Shouldn't Be Doing This
Words and music by Jim Lauderdale.
Mighty Nice Music, 1998/Blue Water, 1998/Hornbill Music, 1998.
Best-selling record by George Strait from the album *One Step at a Time* (MCA Nashville, 98).

We Shall Overcome
Words and music by Traditional.
Ludlow Music Inc., 1945.
Revived by Bruce Springsteen on the album *Where Have All the Flowers Gone: The Songs of Pete Seeger* (Appleseed/Red House, 98).

Weak
Words and music by Robert France, Richard Lewis, Deborah Dyer, and Martin Kent.
Chrysalis Music Group, 1995.
Revived by by Rod Stewart on the album *When We Were the New Boys* (Warner Brothers, 98).

Wedding Night
Words and music by Claibe Richardson and Stephe Cole.
Introduced by the cast of Night of the Hunter on the album *Night of the Hunter* (Varese Sarabande, 98).

Westside
Words and music by Terrance Quaites, TQ Sample, Mike Mosley, R Simmons, Robert Ford, Denzil Miller, James Moore, Kurt Walker, and Femi Ojtunde.
Sony ATV Songs, 1998/EMI-Blackwood Music Inc., 1998/Strictly TQ, 1998/Tickson Music, 1998/Four Knights Music Co., 1998/Neutral Gray Music, 1998/Steady Mobbin', 1998/Music Corp. of America,

1998.
Best-selling record by TQ from the album *They Never Saw Me Coming* (Work/Epic, 98).

What Are Families For
Words and music by Loudon Wainwright.
Snowden Music, 1998.
Introduced by Loudon Wainwright on the album *Little Ship* (Charisma/Virgin, 98).

What If I Said
Words and music by Anita Cochran.
Warner-Tamerlane Music, 1997/Chenowee, 1997.
Best-selling record by Anita Cochran with Steve Wariner from the album *Back to You* (Warner Brothers, 97).

What It's Like
Words and music by Everlast Shrody.
Slack A. D. Music, 1998/T-Boy Music, 1998.
Best-selling record by Everlast from the album *Whitey Ford Sings the Blues* (Tommy Boy, 98).

What Kind of Love Are You On
Words and music by Steven Tyler, Joe Perry, Tommy Shaw, and Jack Blades.
Ranch Rock, 1998/Warner-Tamerlane Music, 1998.
Best-selling record by Aerosmith in the film and on the soundtrack album *Armageddon* (Columbia, 98).

What More Do I Need
Words and music by Stephen Sondheim.
Burthen Music Co., Inc., 1954.
Revived by the Bridewell Theatre Company in the musical and on the cast album *Saturday Night* (RCA, 98).

What the World Needs Now Is Love
Words and music by Burt Bacharach and Hal David.
Casa David, 1967/WB Music, 1967.
Revived by Dionne Warwick and the Hip-Hop Nation United on the album *Dionne Sings Dionne* (River North, 98).

What You Want
Words and music by Mason Betha, Keisha Spivey, Na Mase Myrick, Sean Combs, and Curtis Mayfield.
EMI-April Music, 1997/Peer Pera, 1998/Megawatts, 1998/Tol Muziek, 1997/Warner-Chappell Music, 1997.
Best-selling record by Mase featuring Total from the album *Harlem World* (Bad Boy/Arista, 98).

What's This Life For
Words and music by Scott Stapp and Mark Tremonti.
Stapp/Tremonti Music, New York, 1998/Dwight Frye, 1998.
Best-selling record by Creed from the album *My Own Prison* (Wind-Up, 98).

Wheels of a Dream
Words and music by Lynn Ahrens and Stephen Flaherty.
WB Music, 1997.
Revived by Frankie Laine on the album *Wheels of a Dream* (After 9/Touchwood, 98).

When I Was a Child (English)
Words and music by Jimmy Page, Robert Plant, Stephen Jones, and Michael Pearson.
WB Music, 1998.
Introduced by Page & Plant on the album *Walking into Clarksville* (Atlantic, 98).

When the Lights Go Out (English)
Words and music by Elliott Kennedy, Tim Lever, Mike Percy, John Mclaughlin, and Five.
Windswept Pacific, 1998.
Best-selling record by Five from the album *5* (Arista, 98).

When the Rainbow Comes (English)
Words and music by Karl Wallinger.
Polygram International Music, 1985.
Revived by Shawn Colvin in the film and on the soundtrack album *Armageddon* (Columbia/Sony Music Soundtrax, 98).

When We Ran
Words and music by John Hiatt.
Careers-BMG Music, 1985.
Revived by Linda Ronstadt on the album *We Ran* (Elektra, 98).

When You Believe
Words and music by Babyface (pseudonym for Kenny Edwards) and Stephen Schwartz.
Cherry Lane Music Co., 1998/Cherry River Music Co., 1998.
Introduced by Whitney Houston and Mariah Carey in the film and on the soundtrack album *The Prince of Egypt* (Dream Works, 98). Won an Academy Award for Best Song of the Year, 1998.

When You Grow Up You'll Know
Words and music by Alan Jay Lerner and Burton Lane.
Chappell & Co., Inc., 1998.
Revived by Brock Peters on the album *Lerner, Loewe, Lane & Friends* (Varese Sarabande, 98). From the unproduced film *Huckleberry Finn*.

Where the Boys Are
Words and music by Neil Sedaka and Howard Greenfield.
Careers-BMG Music, 1961/Windswept Pacific, 1961/Screen Gems-EMI Music Inc., 1961.
Revived by Linda Imperial (Interhit, 98).

Where the Green Grass Grows
Words and music by Jess Leary and Craig Wiseman.
Song Matters Music, 1997/Famous Music Corp., 1997/Almo Music Corp., 1997/Daddy Rabbitt Music, 1997.
Best-selling record by Tim McGraw from the album *Everywhere* (Curb, 97).

Where Have All the Flowers Gone
Words and music by Pete Seeger.
Sanga Music Inc., 1961.
Revived by Pete Seeger on the album *The Songs of Pete Seeger* (Appleseed, 98).

Whiskey on the Wound
Words and music by Leslie Satcher.
EMI Music Publishing, 1998/Song Island Music, 1998.
Introduced by Pam Tillis on the album *Every Time* (Arista Nashville, 98).

Who Would Have Thought
Words and music by Tim Armstrong.
Dr. Benway Music, 1998.
Introduced by Rancid on the album *Life Won't Wait* (Epitaph, 98).

Why Can't This Be Love
Words and music by Eddie Van Halen, Alex Van Halen, Michael Anthony, and Sammy Hagar.
WB Music, 1986.
Revived by Gigolo Aunts on the album *Everybody Wants Some: A Loose Interpretation of the Musical Genius of Van Halen* (CherryDisc/Roadrunner, 98).

Why Do I Lie
Words and music by Jill Cuniff, Kathy Schellenbach, and Viv Trimble.
EMI-April Music, 1997.
Revived by Luscious Jackson in the film and on the soundtrack album *Good Will Hunting* (Capitol, 97).

Wide Open Spaces
Words and music by Susan Gibson.
Groobee, Amarillo, 1998/Pie Eyed Groobie, 1998.
Best-selling record by the Dixie Chicks from the album *Wide Open Spaces* (Monument, 98).

Wish I Were You
Words and music by Patty Smyth-McEnroe and Glen Burtnik.
EMI-Blackwood Music Inc., 1998/Pink Smoke Music, 1998/War Bride
Music, 1998.
Introduced by Patty Smyth in the film and on the soundtrack album
Armageddon (Columbia/Sony Music Soundtrax, 98).

Wishful Thinking
Words and music by Duncan Sheik.
Careers-BMG Music, 1997/Fox Film Music Corp., 1997.
Introduced by Duncan Sheik in the film and on the soundtrack album
Great Expectations (Atlantic, 97).

Wishing on a Star
Words and music by Billy Calvin.
Warner-Tamerlane Music, 1977.
Revived by Tina Marie on the TV show *New York Undercover* and
featured on the album *New York Undercover: A Night at Natalie's*
(MCA, 98).

Wishlist
Words and music by Eddie Vedder.
Innocent Bystander Music, 1998.
Best-selling record by Pearl Jam from the album *Yield* (Epic, 98).

Witches Rave
Words and music by Jeff Buckley.
El Viejito, 1998/Sony ATV Songs, 1998.
Introduced by Jeff Buckley on the album *Sketches (For My Sweetheart
the Drunk)* (Columbia, 98).

Wonder Why We Ever Go Home
Words and music by Jimmy Buffett.
Duchess Music Corp., 1975/Unart Music Corp., 1975.
Introduced by Jimmy Buffett in the film and on the soundtrack album
Rancho Deluxe (Rykodisc, 98).

Wonderful Remark (Irish)
Words and music by Van Morrison.
Caledonia Soul Music, 1983/WB Music, 1983.
Revived by Van Morrison on the album *The Philosopher's Stone*
(Polydor/A & M, 98).

Woolie Bullie
Words and music by Dave Thomas.
Polygram Music Publishing Inc., 1998.
Introduced by Pere Ubu on the album *Pennsylvania* (Tim Kerr/Capitol,
98).

Y

You Are My Home
Words and music by Diane Warren.
Realsongs, 1998.
Introduced by Vanessa Williams and Chayanne in the film and on the
soundtrack album *Dance with Me* (Epic/Sony Soundtrax, 98).

You & Me & the Bottle Makes Three Tonight (Baby)
Words and music by Scotty Morris.
Big Bad Voodoo Music, Ventura, 1996.
Revived by Big Bad Voodoo Daddy on the album *Swing This, Baby*
(Slimstyle/Beyond, 98).

You Move Me
Words and music by Gordon Kennedy and Pierce Pettis.
Polygram International Music, 1998/Piercepettisongs Music, 1998.
Best-selling record by Garth Brooks from the album *Sevens* (Capitol
Nashville, 98).

You Were There
Words and music by Babyface (pseudonym for Kenny Edmunds).
Ecaf Music, 1998/Sony ATV Songs, 1998.
Introduced by Babyface in the film and on the soundtrack album *Simon
Birch* (Epic, 98).

You Won't Forget Me (German)
English words and music by Franz Reuther, Lane McCray, and Peter
Bischof-Fallenstein.
FMP Music, 1998/BMG Songs Inc., 1998.
Best-selling record by La Bouche from the album *S.O.S.* (RCA, 98).

Your Good Girl's Gonna Go Bad
Words and music by Billy Sherrill and Glenn Sutton.
EMI Music Publishing, 1967/Al Gallico Music Corp., 1967.
Revived by K.T. Oslin on the album *Tammy Wynette: Remembered*
(Asylum, 98).

Your Imagination
Words and music by Brian Wilson, James Peterik, Joseph Thomas, and Stephen Dahl.
New Executive Music, 1998/On the Fox, 1998.
Best-selling record by Brian Wilson from the album *Imagination* (Paladin/Giant/Warner Brothers, 98).

Your Life Is Now
Words and music by John Mellencamp and George Greene.
Katsback Music, 1998/Little B, 1998.
Best-selling record by John Mellencamp from the album *Your Life Is Now* (Columbia, 98).

You're Beginning to Get to Me
Words and music by Tom Shapiro and Aaron Barker.
Hamstein Cumberland, Nashville, 1998/O-Tex Music, 1998/Blind Sparrow Music, 1998/Sony ATV Songs, 1998.
Best-selling record by Clay Walker from the album *Rumor Has It* (Giant/Warner Brothers, 98).

You're the Boss
Words and music by Jerry Leiber and Mike Stoller.
Jerry Leiber Music, 1964/Mike Stoller Music, 1964.
Revived by The Brian Setzer Orchestra with Gwen Stefani on the album *The Dirty Boogie* (Interscope, 98).

You're Easy on the Eyes
Words and music by Tom Shapiro, Chris Waters, and Terri Clark.
Hamstein Cumberland, Nashville, 1998/Sony ATV Tree Publishing, 1998/Chris Waters Music, 1998/Polygram International Music, 1998/ Terri Ooo, 1998.
Best-selling record by Terri Clark from the album *How It Feels* (Mercury, 98).

You're Gone
Words and music by John Vezner and Paul Williams.
Warner-Tamerlane Music, 1998/Minnesota Man, 1998/WB Music, 1998/ Hillabeans, 1998.
Best-selling record by Diamond Rio from the album *Diamond Rio: Greatest Hits* (Arista Nashville, 98).

You're Still the One (Canadian-English)
Words and music by Shania Twain and Robert John Lange.
Songs of Polygram, 1997/Loon Echo Music, 1997/Zomba Music, 1997.
Best-selling record by Shania Twain from the album *Come On Over* (Mercury, 97). Won a Grammy Award for Best Country Song of the Year, 1998. Nominated for Grammy Awards, Best Record of the Year, 1998 and Best Song of the Year, 1998.

You've Got to Talk to Me
Words and music by Jamie O'Hara.
Sony ATV Tree Publishing, 1997/Manticore Music, 1997.
Best-selling record by Lee Ann Womack from the album *Lee Ann Womack* (Decca Nashville, 98).

Z

Zoot Suit Riot
Words and music by Steve Perry.
Famous Music Corp., 1998.
Best-selling record by Cherry Poppin' Daddies from the album *Cherry Poppin' Daddies* (Mojo/Universal, 98).

Lyricists & Composers Index

Lyricists & Composers Index

Lyricists & Composers Index

Lyricists & Composers Index

Lyricists & Composers Index

Lyricists & Composers Index

Lyricists & Composers Index

Lyricists & Composers Index

Sweat, Keith
  Come and Get with Me
Sweet, Jody
  Lonely Won't Leave Me Alone
Syles, David
  Money, Power & Respect
Tate, Danny
  Somehow, Somewhere, Someway
Taylor, Bobby
  A Man Holdin' On (to a Woman
  Lettin' Go)
Taylor, Samuel
  Get at Me Dog
Tejeda, Japhe
  The Boy Is Mine
  Still Not a Player
Tesh, John
  Give Me Forever (I Do)
Thomas, Dave
  Woolie Bullie
Thomas, Joe
  Still Not a Player
Thomas, Joseph
  South American
  Your Imagination
Thomas, Peter
  This Is Hardcore
Thomas, Rob
  Real World
Thompson, Wayne Carson
  Horse Called Music
Thornally, Phil
  Torn
Thornley, Ian
  The Oaf (My Life Is Wasted)
Tirro, John
  Imagine That
Tolbert, Tony
  I Still Love You
Traditional
  We Shall Overcome
Trahan, Charles
  U Like Pina Coladas
Trask, Stephen
  Midnight Radio
Tremonti, Mark
  What's This Life For

Tribble, Kim
  I Can Still Feel You
Tricky
  Broken Homes
Trimble, Viv
  Why Do I Lie
Trott, Jeff
  My Favorite Mistake
Tucker, Patrick
  Because of You
Turner, Zack
  Texas Size Heartache
Twain, Shania
  From This Moment On
  Honey I'm Home
  You're Still the One
Twink
  Do It
Tyler, Steven
  What Kind of Love Are You On
Ulrich, Lars
  Better Than You
  Fuel
  The Unforgiven II
Usher, Gary
  In My Room
Van Halen, Alex
  Fire in the Hole
  Jump
  Why Can't This Be Love
Van Halen, Eddie
  Fire in the Hole
  Jump
  Why Can't This Be Love
Van Zandt, Townes
  If I Needed You
Vandross, Luther
  Love Me
Vassar, Phil
  Bye Bye
  I'm Alright
  Little Red Rodeo
  Right on the Money
Vaughan, Sharon
  Out of My Bones
Vaughn, Ben
  In the Street

Lyricists & Composers Index

Important Performances Index

Songs are listed under the works in which they were introduced or given significant renditions. The index is organized into major sections by performance medium: Album, Movie, Musical, Performer, Revue, Television Show.

Album

Alabama Song
  Alabama Song
  Is Heaven Good Enough for You
  A Soft Place to Fall
All Saints
  Lady Marmelade
  Never Ever
All the Pain That Money Can Buy
  The Way
All Work No Play
  Body Bumpin' Yippie Yi-Yo
Americana
  Pretty Fly (For a White Guy)
And Then There Was Bass
  U Like Pina Coladas
Angels with Dirty Faces
  Broken Homes
Aquemini
  Rosa Parks
Armageddon
  I Don't Want to Miss a Thing
  Leaving on a Jet Plane
  What Kind of Love Are You On
  When the Rainbow Comes
  Wish I Were You

Ava Adore
  Ava Adore
  For Martha
  Perfect
  Tear
Babe-Pig in the City
  That'll Do
Baby One More Time
  ...Baby One More Time
Back to You
  What If I Said
Back with a Heart
  I Honestly Love You
  Love Is a Gift
Backstreet Boys
  Everybody (Backstreet's Back)
  I'll Never Break Your Heart
Baseketball
  Take on Me
Bass All-Stars
  Time After Time
Bathhouse Bette
  Boxing
  I'm Hip
  My One True Friend
Before These Crowded Streets
  Don't Drink the Water

123

Important Performances Index — Album

132

Musical

Important Performances Index — Performer

Television Show

Awards Index

A list of songs nominated for Academy Awards by the Academy of Motion Picture Arts and Sciences and Grammy Awards from the National Academy of Recording Arts and Sciences. Asterisks indicate the winners; multiple listings indicate multiple nominations.

1998

Academy Award
I Don't Want to Miss a Thing
The Prayer
A Soft Place to Fall
That'll Do
When You Believe*

Grammy Award
All My Life
Bitter Sweet Symphony
The Boy Is Mine
Celebrity Skin
Closing Time
Doo Wop (That Thing)*
Have a Little Faith in Me
Holes in the Floor of Heaven
I Don't Want to Miss a Thing
If You Ever Have Forever in Mind
Iris
Lean on Me
My Heart Will Go On*
Ray of Light
A Rose Is Still a Rose
This Kiss
To Make You Feel My Love
Uninvited*
You're Still the One
You're Still the One*

List of Publishers

A directory of publishers of the songs included in *Popular Music, 1998*. Publishers that are members of the American Society of Composers, Authors, and Publishers or whose catalogs are available under ASCAP license are indicated by the designation (ASCAP). Publishers that have granted performing rights to Broadcast Music, Inc., are designated by the notation (BMI). Publishers whose catalogs are represented by The Society of Composers, Authors and Music Publishers of Canada, are indicated by the designation (SOCAN). Publishers whose catalogs are represented by SESAC, Inc., are indicated by the designation (SESAC).

The addresses were gleaned from a variety of sources, including ASCAP, BMI, SOCAN, SESAC, and *Billboard* magazine. As in any volatile industry, many of the addresses may become outdated quickly. In the interim between the book's completion and its subsequent publication, some publishers may have been consolidated into others or changed hands. This is a fact of life long endured by the music business and its constituents. The data collected here, and throughout the book, are as accurate as such circumstances allow.

A

David Aaron Music (ASCAP)
see Sony ATV Tree Publishing

ABKCO Music Inc. (BMI)
1700 Broadway
New York, New York 10019

About Time
see Warner-Chappell Music

Acuff Rose Music (BMI)
65 Music Square West
Nashville, Tennessee 37203

Additions Hate (ASCAP)
see EMI Music Publishing

Aerostation Corp. (ASCAP)
16214 Morrison St.
Encino, California 91436

Air Chrysalis Scandinavia
see Chrysalis Music Group

Air Control Music (ASCAP)
see EMI Music Publishing

All About Me (BMI)
see Warner-Chappell Music

147

List of Publishers

All Seeing Eye (ASCAP)
see Warner-Chappell Music

Alley Music (BMI)
1619 Broadway, 11th Fl.
New York, New York 10019

Almo/Irving
1358 N. LaBrea
Los Angeles, California 90028

Almo/Irving Music (BMI)
1358 N La Brea
Los Angeles, California 90028

Almo Music Corp. (BMI)
360 N. La Cienega
Los Angeles, California 90048

Amadeus (ASCAP)
c/o Frank, Weinrib, Rudell & Vassal
488 Madison Ave., 8th Fl.
New York, New York 10022

Amokshasong (ASCAP)
see EMI Music Publishing

Anotation (ASCAP)
see Warner-Chappell Music

Antisia Music Inc. (ASCAP)
183 Jonathan Dr.
Stamford, Connecticut 06903

Anwa Music (ASCAP)
see Rondor Music Inc.

Areles (BMI)
see Warner-Chappell Music

Aresti Arrangements (BMI)
see Warner-Chappell Music

Armacien Music (BMI)
see Warner-Chappell Music

Aruba (ASCAP)
see EMI Music Publishing

Arzo Music (ASCAP)
110 W. 57th St., 7th Fl.
New York, New York 10019

ATV Music Corp. (BMI)
see MCA, Inc.

Audre Mae Music (BMI)
34 Dogwood Dr.
Smithtown, New York 11787

B

Baba Jinde (ASCAP)
see EMI Music Publishing

Baby Dumplin' (BMI)
see Almo/Irving Music

Baby Mae Music (BMI)
c/o Hamstein
PO Box 163870
Austin, Texas 78716

Balmur Music (Canada) (SESAC)
Address Unavailable

Barricade Music Inc. (ASCAP)
see Almo Music Corp.

Jeff Barry Music (ASCAP)
c/o Jeff Barry
544 Bellagio Terrace
Los Angeles, California 90049

Basically Zappo Music (ASCAP)
see Warner-Chappell Music

Be Le Be (ASCAP)
see Warner-Chappell Music

Benefit Music (BMI)
7250 Beverly Blvd
Los Angeles, California 90036

Bernard's Other Music (BMI)
see Warner-Chappell Music

BGG (SOCAN)
Address Unavailable

Craig Bickhardt Music
see Almo/Irving

Bidnis Inc Music (BMI)
see EMI Music Publishing

Bienstock Publishing Co. (ASCAP)
see Alley Music

Big Bad Voodoo Music (ASCAP)
PO Box 2146
Ventura, California 93002

Big Ears Music Inc. (ASCAP)
see Bughouse

Big Giant Music (BMI)
see Warner-Chappell Music

Big P Music (BMI)
1651 South Lubdill, No. 102178
Baton Rouge, Louisiana 70806

Big Picture (BMI)
see EMI Music Publishing

Big Tooth Music Corp. (ASCAP)
see Chrysalis Music Group

Bipa (ASCAP)
see Warner-Chappell Music

Biscuits and Gravy Music (BMI)
see Warner-Chappell Music

Black Fountain (ASCAP)
see BMG Music

Black Lava (ASCAP)
23275 Sylvann St.
Woodland Hills, California 91367

Blackened Music (BMI)
c/o Prager & Fenton
12424 Wilshire Blvd., Ste. 1000
Los Angeles, California 90025

Blind Sparrow Music (BMI)
see Sony ATV Music

Bloody Heavy (BMI)
see Dinger & Ollie Music

Blue Book Music (BMI)
1225 N. Chester Ave.
Bakersfield, California 93308

Helene Blue (ASCAP)
see Warner-Chappell Music

Blue Sky Rider Songs (BMI)
c/o Prager and Fenton
6363 Sunset Blvd., Ste. 706
Los Angeles, California 90028

Blue Water (BMI)
see Mighty Nice Music

BMG Music (ASCAP)
1540 Broadway
New York, New York 10036

BMG Songs Inc. (ASCAP)
8370 Wilshire Blvd.
Beverly Hills, California 90211

BNC (ASCAP)
see Almo/Irving Music

Boomer X (ASCAP)
c/o Earl Simmons
138 Elm St.
Mt. Vernon, New York 11055

Rory Bourke (BMI)
see EMI Music Publishing

The Bourne Co. (ASCAP)
5 W. 37th St.
New York, New York 10018

Bow Down (ASCAP)
see EMI Music Publishing

Bri-Murn Music (BMI)
Address Unavailable

Brian's Dream (ASCAP)
see Sony ATV Music

Edie Brickell Songs (ASCAP)
see MCA, Inc.

Bro N' Sis Music (BMI)
see Keith Sykes Music

Brooklyn Dust Music (ASCAP)
c/o Kenneth B. Anderson, Esq.
Loeb & Loeb
230 Park Ave.
New York, New York 10169

List of Publishers

Brother 4 Brothers (ASCAP)
see Warner-Chappell Music

Jess Brown (ASCAP)
see Almo/Irving Music

Jameison Brown Music (BMI)
see Mike Curb Productions

Bruised Oranges (BMI)
4121 Wilshire Blvd., Ste. 5204
Los Angeles, California 10017

Budget (BMI)
see Bug Music

Bug Music (BMI)
Bug Music Group
6777 Hollywood Blvd., 9th Fl.
Hollywood, California 90028

Bughouse (ASCAP)
c/o Bug Music Group
6777 Hollywood Blvd., 9th Floor
Hollywood, California 90028

Built on Rock Music (ASCAP)
see Ensign Music

Bull God (BMI)
see Polygram Music Publishing Inc.

Gary Burr Music (BMI)
see Tree Publishing Co., Inc.

Burrin Avenue Music (BMI)
6430 Sunset Blvd., Ste 900
Hollywood, California 90028

Burthen Music Co., Inc. (ASCAP)
see Chappell & Co., Inc.

C

Caledonia Soul Music (ASCAP)
see WB Music

Cameo5 (ASCAP)
see Warner-Chappell Music

Camex Music Inc. (BMI)
489 5th Ave.
New York, New York 10017

C'amore (BMI)
see Chrysalis Music Group

Shawn Camp (BMI)
see Sony ATV Music

Carbert Music Inc. (BMI)
1619 Broadway, Rm. 609
New York, New York 10019

Careers-BMG Music
see BMG Music

Wayne Carson (BMI)
c/o Richard Joseph
116 N. Robertson Blvd., Ste. 705
Los Angeles, California 90048

Joe Cartegena (ASCAP)
see Almo/Irving Music

Cartertunes (ASCAP)
132 Haud Ave.
Cornwall, New York 12518

Casa David (ASCAP)
c/o Hal David
12711 Ventura Blvd., Ste. 420
Studio City, California 91604

Chappell & Co., Inc. (ASCAP)
see Warner-Chappell Music

Cheiron Music (ASCAP)
see Zomba Music

Chenowee (BMI)
see Warner-Chappell Music

Cherry Lane Music Co. (ASCAP)
6 E. 32nd St., 11th Fl.
New York, New York 10016

Cherry River Music Co. (BMI)
see Cherry Lane Music Co.

Chicken on Fire (BMI)
see Bug Music

Chicksaw Roan Music (BMI)
see Texas Wedge Music

Chrome Dog (ASCAP)
see Polygram Music Publishing Inc.

Chrysalis Music Group (ASCAP)
9255 Sunset Blvd., No. 319
Los Angeles, California 90069

Chyna Baby Music (BMI)
see EMI Music Publishing

Cina (BMI)
see Warner-Chappell Music

Cinderful Music (BMI)
see Chrysalis Music Group

Clement Family (BMI)
see Jack Clement Music, Inc.

Jack Clement Music, Inc. (BMI)
639 Madison Ave.
Memphis, Tennessee 38103

CMI America (ASCAP)
1102 17th Ave. S.
Nashville, Tennessee 37212

Coal Dust West (BMI)
c/o William Coben
2029 Century Park
Los Angeles, California 90067

Cody River Music (ASCAP)
15030 Ventura Blvd., Ste. 3535
Sherman Oaks, California 91403

Colden Grey Music (ASCAP)
Grubman, Indursky, Schindler & Gold
152 W. 57th St.
New York, New York 10019

Colgems-EMI Music (ASCAP)
see EMI Music Publishing

Tom Collins Music Corp. (BMI)
Box 121407
Nashville, Tennessee 37212

Colter Bay Music (BMI)
see Almo Music Corp.

Janice Combs Music (ASCAP)
see EMI Music Publishing

Justin Combs Music (ASCAP)
see EMI Music Publishing

Common Green Music (BMI)
see Rondor Music Inc.

Computer Chance (ASCAP)
see Warner-Chappell Music

Congregation (SESAC)
see Rick Hall Music

Constant Pressure Music (BMI)
see Warner-Chappell Music

Controversy Music (ASCAP)
c/o Ziffren Brittenham & Branca
2121 Ave. of the Stars
Los Angeles, California 90067

Cooch & Hooch (BMI)
see Famous Music Corp.

Copyright Management Inc. (BMI)
1102 17th Ave So.
Nashville, Tennessee 37082

Copyright Service Bureau Ltd.
221 W. 57th St.
New York, New York 10019

Coral Reefer Music (BMI)
c/o Gelfand, Rennert & Feldman
Attn: Babbie Green
1880 Century Park, E., No. 900
Los Angeles, California 90067

Cord Kayla Music (ASCAP)
see EMI Music Publishing

Vanessa Corish (BMI)
see MCA Music

Chris Cornell (ASCAP)
see TCF Music

Corner of Clark and Kent (BMI)
see EMI Music Publishing

List of Publishers

Cotillion Music Inc. (BMI)
75 Rockefeller Plaza, 2nd Fl.
New York, New York 10019

Cracklin' Music (BMI)
see Bug Music

Crazy Crow Music (BMI)
see Siquomb Publishing Corp.

Creation Music (BMI)
see Sony ATV Music

Creeping Death Music (ASCAP)
c/o Manatt Phelps Rothenberg & Tunn
ey
11355 W. Olympic Blvd.
Los Angeles, California 90064

Mike Curb Productions (BMI)
948 Tourmaline Dr.
Newbury Park, California 91220

Cyanide Breathmint Music (ASCAP)
see BMG Music

D

Da Ish (ASCAP)
see EMI Music Publishing

Daddy Rabbitt Music (ASCAP)
see Almo/Irving

Leshawn Daniels (BMI)
see EMI Music Publishing

Danor Music Inc. (BMI)
see Irving Music Inc.

D.A.R.P. Music (ASCAP)
see Diva One

Dee Cam Publishing (ASCAP)
303 Talbert Ave.
Santa Rosa, California 95445

Def Jam Music (ASCAP)
160 Varick St.
New York, New York 10013

Demenoid Deluxe Music (ASCAP)
see Warner-Chappell Music

Desmophobia (ASCAP)
see Polygram Music Publishing Inc.

D'extraordinary (ASCAP)
see Warner-Chappell Music

Diamond Mine (ASCAP)
see Little Shop of Morgansongs

Diamond Three (BMI)
see Starstruck Writers Group

Dinger & Ollie Music (BMI)
see Duke T

Walt Disney Music (ASCAP)
500 S. Buena Vista St.
Burbank, California 91521

Diva One (ASCAP)
Gelfand, Rennert & Feldman
c/o Michael Bivens
1880 Century Park E., Ste. 900
Los Angeles, California 90067

Divided (BMI)
see Zomba House

Divine Pimp Music (ASCAP)
see BMG Music

Dixie Stars (ASCAP)
see Hori Pro Entertainment Group

Dixie Stars Music (ASCAP)
see Hori Pro Entertainment Group

DJ Irv (BMI)
see EMI Music Publishing

Do What I Gotta Music (ASCAP)
see EMI Music Publishing

Dr. Benway Music (BMI)
c/o Phillips, Mizer, Benjamin & Kri
Attn: Rosemary Carroll
40 W. 57th St.
New York, New York 10019

152

Dog Dream (ASCAP)
Box 483
Newton Centre, Massachusetts 02159

Doors Music Co. (ASCAP)
c/o Greene & Reynolds
8200 Sunset Blvd., No. 706
Los Angeles, California 90069

Downright Dizzy (ASCAP)
see EMI Music Publishing

Draco Cornelius (ASCAP)
see Polygram Music Publishing Inc.

Dreamworks (BMI)
Address Unavailable

Dub Notes
23 E. Lancaster Ave.
Ardmore, Pennsylvania 19003

Dub's World Music (ASCAP)
see MCA Music

Duchess Music Corp. (BMI)
1755 Broadway, 8th Fl.
New York, New York 10019

Dujuan (BMI)
see Zomba Music

Duke T (BMI)
11355 W. Olympic Blvd.
Los Angeles, California 90064

E

Early Morning Music (ASCAP)
Division of EMP Ltd.
350 Davenport Rd.
Toronto, Ontario 180
Canada

Ecaf Music (BMI)
see Sony ATV Music

ECG (BMI)
see Zomba Music

El Viejito (BMI)
see Sony ATV Music

EMI-April Music (ASCAP)
see EMI Music Publishing

EMI-Blackwood Music Inc. (BMI)
see EMI Music Publishing

EMI-Intertrax Music (BMI)
see EMI Music Publishing

EMI Music Publishing
810 7th Ave.
New York, New York 10019

EMI Songs Ltd.
see EMI Music Publishing

EMI U Catalogue (ASCAP)
see EMI Music Publishing

EMI United Catalogue (BMI)
see EMI Music Publishing

Enlightened Kitty (ASCAP)
see MCA, Inc.

Ensign Music (BMI)
see Famous Music Corp.

Erika (ASCAP)
see Warner-Chappell Music

Essex Music International (ASCAP)
see EMI Music Publishing

Evergleam Music (BMI)
see Rondor Music Inc.

Everyone Craves (ASCAP)
see EMI Music Publishing

F

Fake and Jaded (BMI)
see Southfield Road

Famous Music Corp. (ASCAP)
10635 Santa Monica Blvd.
Ste. 300
Los Angeles, California 90025

Farm Hand (ASCAP)
see EMI Music Publishing

153

List of Publishers

Farrenuff (BMI)
see Windswept Pacific

Fat Wax (ASCAP)
see EMI Music Publishing

Feedbach Music (ASCAP)
see Full Keel Music

Felder Pomus (BMI)
see Warner-Chappell Music

Five Cowboys (BMI)
see Sony ATV Music

Flames of Albion Music, Inc. (ASCAP)
Attn: Stevens H. Weiss
34 Pheasant Run
Old Westbury, New York 11568

Fleetwood Mac Music Ltd. (BMI)
315 S. Beverly Dr., Ste. 210
Beverly Hills, California 90212

Floyd's Dream Music (ASCAP)
see BMG Music

Flybridge (BMI)
see EMI Music Publishing

Flying Earform (BMI)
see EMI Music Publishing

Flyte Tyme Tunes (ASCAP)
c/o Margo Matthews
Box 92004
Los Angeles, California 90009

FMP Music
see Warner-Chappell Music

Folkways Music Publishers, Inc.
see TRO-Folkways Music Publishers, Inc.

Foray (SESAC)
see EMI Music Publishing

Foreshadow Songs, Inc. (BMI)
PO Box 120657
Nashville, Tennessee 37212

Foreva (ASCAP)
see Famous Music Corp.

45 Music
Address Unavailable

Four Knights Music Co. (BMI)
see MCA Music

Fox Film Music Corp. (BMI)
c/o Twentieth Century Fox Film Corp
PO Box 900
Beverly Hills, California 90213

Fox-Gimbel Productions (BMI)
c/o Mr. Sidney Aron
10 E. 40th St.
New York, New York 10016

Len Freedman Music
123 El Paseo
Santa Barbara, California 93101

Fresh Avery Music (BMI)
see Sony ATV Music

Dwight Frye (BMI)
Address Unavailable

Full Keel Music (ASCAP)
9320 Wilshire Blvd., Ste. 200
Beverly Hills, California 90212

Full Pull (BMI)
see Windswept Pacific

Funky Noise (ASCAP)
see Famous Music Corp.

Richie Furay (BMI)
see Ten-East Music

G

G. P. Brown Publishing (BMI)
333 Market St.
San Francisco, California 94105

Al Gallico Music Corp. (BMI)
9301 Wilshire, Ste. 311
Beverly Hills, California 90210

Gambi Music Inc. (BMI)
see Copyright Service Bureau Ltd.

Garden Angel (BMI)
see Warner-Chappell Music

Garden Court Music Co. (ASCAP)
Box 1098
Alexandria, Ontario K0C 1A0
Canada

Gavadima Music Inc. (ASCAP)
Peter C. Bennett, Esq.
9060 Santa Monica Blvd., Ste. 300
Los Angeles, California 90069

Gear Publishing (ASCAP)
Division of Hideout Productions
567 Purdy
Birmingham, Michigan 48009

Geffen Music (ASCAP)
see MCA, Inc.

Gem (ASCAP)
see EMI Music Publishing

Genro's Mood (ASCAP)
see EMI Music Publishing

Ghetto Bells Music (BMI)
see Bug Music

Gibb Brothers Music (BMI)
see BMG Music

Gimme Back My Publishing (ASCAP)
see Warner-Chappell Music

Glitterfish (BMI)
see MCA Music

Gnat Booty Music (ASCAP)
see Camex Music Inc.

Godhap Music (BMI)
see EMI Music Publishing

Golden Phoenix (SOCAN)
Address Unavailable

Golden World (ASCAP)
Box 1142
Desert Hot Springs, California 92240

Gooby (BMI)
see Copyright Management Inc.

Good (ASCAP)
see Foreshadow Songs, Inc.

Goodie Mob Music (BMI)
see Organized Noize

Granary Music (BMI)
c/o Linda Clark
PO Box 1304
Burbank, California 91507

Grantsville (ASCAP)
see Zomba Music

Groobee (BMI)
A Division of Groobee Entertainment
2041 S. Travis
Amarillo, Texas 79109

Gunz (BMI)
see EMI Music Publishing

Woody Guthrie Publications (BMI)
see Ludlow Music Inc.

H

Hair Sucker (BMI)
see Sony ATV Music

Rick Hall Music (ASCAP)
PO Box 2527
603 E. Avalon Ave.
Muscle Shoals, Alabama 35662

Hamstein Cumberland (BMI)
1033 18th Ave. S.
Nashville, Tennessee 37212

Heartworm (BMI)
see EMI Music Publishing

Andy Heath (BMI)
see Polygram Music Publishing Inc.

Heathalee (BMI)
see EMI Music Publishing

List of Publishers

Hee Bee Doinit (ASCAP)
see EMI Music Publishing

Herald Square Music Co. (ASCAP)
attn: Freddy Bientetock
1619 Broadway
New York, New York 10019

Herbilicious Music (ASCAP)
see Warner-Chappell Music

HGL Music (ASCAP)
see MCA Music

Hidden Words (BMI)
see Acuff Rose Music

Hideout Records/Distributing Co. (ASCAP)
see Gear Publishing

High and Dry (BMI)
see Bug Music

Hinayana (BMI)
see EMI Music Publishing

Hingface Music (BMI)
see Ensign Music

Hip Chic (ASCAP)
see Warner-Chappell Music

Hit Co. South (ASCAP)
see Sony ATV Music

Holmes Line of Music (ASCAP)
228 W. 71st St.
New York, New York 10023

Hook Mo (BMI)
see Polygram Music Publishing Inc.

Hori Pro Entertainment Group (ASCAP)
1819 Broadway
Nashville, Tennessee 37203

Hornbill Music (BMI)
see Polygram Music Publishing Inc.

Horrible (BMI)
see EMI Music Publishing

Hot Churro (BMI)
see Bug Music

House of Cash Inc. (BMI)
c/o Reba Hancock
Box 508
Hendersonville, Tennessee 37077

House of Fun Music (BMI)
1348 Lexington Ave.
New York, New York 10128

House Notes Music (BMI)
see New Haven Music

Melanie Howard (ASCAP)
see Big Giant Music

Howcutt (BMI)
see Almo/Irving Music

Human Boy Music (ASCAP)
see Warner-Chappell Music

I

I Heard Them (BMI)
see MCA Music

If Dreams Had Wings (ASCAP)
c/o CMRRA
56 Wellesley St., W.
Toronto, Ontario M5S 2S4
Canada

Indian Love Bride Music (ASCAP)
Siegel, Feldstein, Duffin, & Vuylst
1500 Broadway, Ste. 1400
New York, New York 10036

Innocent Bystander Music (ASCAP)
207 1/2 1st Ave. S.
Seattle, Washington 98104

Insongnia (BMI)
28908 Grayfox St.
Malibu, California 90265

Instantly (ASCAP)
see Warner-Chappell Music

Irving Music Inc. (BMI)
  360 N. LaCienega Blvd.
  Los Angeles, California 90048

J

Ja (BMI)
  see EMI Music Publishing

Jae'wans Music (BMI)
  see EMI Music Publishing

Jamron (ASCAP)
  see BMG Music

Jelly's Jams L.L.C. Music (BMI)
  see EMI Music Publishing

Jimi-Lane Music (BMI)
  PO Box 5295, Ocean Park Sta.
  Santa Monica, California 90405

JMM Music (BMI)
  see Of Music

Jobete Music Co. (ASCAP)
  attn: Denise Maurin
  6255 Sunset Blvd.
  Los Angeles, California 90028

Joe's Cafe (BMI)
  see Famous Music Corp.

Lucy Jones Music (BMI)
  see Warner-Chappell Music

Hudson Jordan (ASCAP)
  see Wixen Music

Steven A. Jordan Music (ASCAP)
  see EMI Music Publishing

Juicy Time (ASCAP)
  see EMI Music Publishing

Jumping Bean Music (ASCAP)
  see EMI Music Publishing

Jumping Cat Music (ASCAP)
  see Write Treatage Music

K

Kababa Music (ASCAP)
  c/o Pen Music Group
  6255 Sunset Blvd., Ste. 1024
  Los Angeles, California 90028-7407

Kalinmia (ASCAP)
  see EMI Music Publishing

Keel/Ko (ASCAP)
  see EMI Music Publishing

R. Kelly Music (BMI)
  see Zomba Music

Kerrion (BMI)
  see Lilly Mack

Kiayasong
  Address Unavailable

Kid Julie (BMI)
  see Red Brazos

Kidbilly (BMI)
  see Red Brazos

Killer Cam (ASCAP)
  see Warner-Chappell Music

May King Poetry Music (BMI)
  see Yam Gruel Music

Kipahulu Music Co. (ASCAP)
  see Screen Gems-EMI Music Inc.

Stephen A. Kipner Music (ASCAP)
  Attn: Stephen A. Kipner
  19646 Valley View Dr.
  Topanga, California 90290

Know Jack (BMI)
  see Famous Music Corp.

Koala Music Inc. (ASCAP)
  30 Highbrook Ave.
  Pelham, New York 10803

Kohaw (ASCAP)
  see Almo/Irving Music

List of Publishers

Kokomo Music (ASCAP)
Attn: Bonnie Raitt
PO Box 626
Los Angeles, California 90078

Krazyie Bone (ASCAP)
see Sony ATV Music

L

A La Mode Music (ASCAP)
c/o Braun, Margolis, Ryan, Burrill
& Besse
attn: Malcolm Wiseman, ESQ
1900 Ave. of the Stars
Los Angeles, California 90067

Jerry Leiber Music (ASCAP)
9000 Sunset Blvd.
Ste. 1107
Los Angeles, California 90069

Les Editions Musicale (ASCAP)
see EMI Music Publishing

Less Than Zero (BMI)
see Southfield Road

Let Me Show You (ASCAP)
Address Unavailable

Lev-a-Tunes (ASCAP)
see Bug Music

Lil Lu Lu Music (BMI)
see EMI Music Publishing

Lilly Mack (BMI)
417 Regent St.
Inglewood, California 90301

Lillywilly (ASCAP)
see Warner-Chappell Music

Hank Linderman (ASCAP)
see EMI Music Publishing

Little Cayman (BMI)
see EMI Music Publishing

Little Duck (SESAC)
see Famous Music Corp.

Little Shop of Morgansongs (BMI)
1102 17th Ave. S.
Nashville, Tennessee 37212

LL Cool J Music (ASCAP)
attn: James Todd Smith
PO Box 219
Elmont, New York 11003

Longitude Music (BMI)
c/o Windswept Pacific Entertainment
9320 Wilshire Blvd., Ste. 200
Beverly Hills, California 91212

Loon Echo Music (BMI)
see Zomba Music

Loud and Vulgar (ASCAP)
see EMI Music Publishing

Ludlow Music Inc. (BMI)
10 Columbus Circle, Ste. 1406
New York, New York 10019

Lushmole Music (BMI)
see EMI Music Publishing

Lympia Music (BMI)
c/o Bug Music
6777 Hollywood Blvd., 9th Fl.
Hollywood, California 90028

M

Maclen Music Inc. (BMI)
see ATV Music Corp.

Magnasong (ASCAP)
see Tom Collins Music Corp.

Major Bob Music (ASCAP)
1109 17th Ave. S
Nashville, Tennessee 37212

Man-Ken Music Ltd. (BMI)
34 Pheasant Run
Old Westbury, New York 11568

Manticore Music (ASCAP)
c/o Arrow, Edelstein, Gross & Margo
919 3rd Ave.
New York, New York 10022

Mark D. Music (BMI)
see Sony ATV Cross Keys Publishing Co.
Inc.

Marshall Law (ASCAP)
see EMI Music Publishing

Mason Betha Music (ASCAP)
see EMI Music Publishing

Mass Confusion Music (ASCAP)
see Warner-Chappell Music

Maypop Music (BMI)
Box 121192e Cavender
702 18th Ave.
Nashville, Tennessee 37212

MCA, Inc. (ASCAP)
1755 Broadway, 8th Fl.
New York, New York 10019

MCA Music (ASCAP)
1755 Broadway
New York, New York 10019

MCA Music Co. Inc. Publishing (SESAC)
see MCA Music

McLaughlin Publishing Co. (BMI)
c/o Mietus Copyright Management
PO Box 432
2351 Laurana Rd.
Union, New Jersey 07083

Dean McTaggart (ASCAP)
see EMI Music Publishing

Ken Meeker (ASCAP)
see EMI Music Publishing

Megawatts (ASCAP)
see EMI Music Publishing

Melody Trails Inc. (BMI)
10 Columbus Circle, Ste. 1406
New York, New York 10019

Micon Publishing (ASCAP)
see EMI Music Publishing

Mighty Nice Music (BMI)
see Polygram Music Publishing Inc.

Milene Music Inc. (ASCAP)
65 Music Square West
Nashville, Tennessee 37203

Dean Miller (ASCAP)
see EMI Music Publishing

Millermo Music (BMI)
see Polygram Music Publishing Inc.

Million Dollar Steve (BMI)
see EMI Music Publishing

Minnesota Man (BMI)
see Warner-Chappell Music

Miss Bessie (ASCAP)
see Warner-Chappell Music

Missoula (BMI)
see EMI Music Publishing

MJ12 Music (BMI)
see EMI Music Publishing

MKD (BMI)
see Famous Music Corp.

Monica's Reluctance to Lob (ASCAP)
see EMI Music Publishing

Monkids (ASCAP)
see Rick Hall Music

Montalupis Music (BMI)
see Rondor Music Inc.

Moo Maison (ASCAP)
see MCA, Inc.

Mood Swing (BMI)
see Wixen Music

Moonlight Canyon (BMI)
see Bug Music

List of Publishers

Rene Moore (ASCAP)
see EMI Music Publishing

Moraine (BMI)
see Famous Music Corp.

Morgan (BMI)
see Little Shop of Morgansongs

Juni Morrison (BMI)
Box 1661
New York, New York 10163

Mother May I (BMI)
15250 Ventura Blvd., Ste. 900
Sherman Oaks, California 91403

MPL Communications Inc. (ASCAP)
c/o Lee Eastman
39 W. 54th St.
New York, New York 10019

Shawn Mullins (BMI)
see EMI Music Publishing

Murlyn (ASCAP)
see Chrysalis Music Group

Music Corp. of America (BMI)
see MCA Music

Music Everyone Craves (BMI)
see Sony ATV Music

Music Force Pacific (BMI)
see Windswept Pacific

Music Impossible (BMI)
see Polygram Music Publishing Inc.

My Own Chit (BMI)
see Warner-Chappell Music

N

Nate Dogg Music (BMI)
see Suge Music

Nate Love's (ASCAP)
see MCA Music

Naughty (ASCAP)
see Jobete Music Co.

Needmore Music (BMI)
4015 5th Ave. S.
Minneapolis, Minnesota 55409

Neon Sky Music (ASCAP)
see EMI Music Publishing

Neutral Gray Music (ASCAP)
405 W. 45th St., No. 4D
New York, New York 10036

New Executive Music (BMI)
c/o Ziffren, Brithenham, Gullen
Attn: John G. Branca
2049 Century Park E., Ste. 2350
Los Angeles, California 90067

New Haven Music (BMI)
see PolyGram Records Inc.

New Nonpariel (BMI)
see Warner-Chappell Music

New Wolf Music (BMI)
see Sony ATV Tree Publishing

Randy Newman Music (ASCAP)
c/o Gelfand, Rennert & Feldman
1880 Century Park, E., Ste. 900
Los Angeles, California 90067

Night Garden Music (BMI)
see Warner-Chappell Music

Glen Nikki (ASCAP)
see Starstruck Writers Group

No Tomato (ASCAP)
see WB Music

Kenny Nolan Publishing (ASCAP)
c/o Peter C. Bennett
503 N. Elm Dr.
Beverly Hills, California 90210

Nomad-Noman Music (BMI)
see Warner-Chappell Music

Norick Music
144 Broad Ave.
Leona, New Jersey 07606

North Avenue (ASCAP)
see EMI Music Publishing

Nothing But the Wolf (BMI)
see Sony ATV Music

Now Sounds Music (BMI)
c/o Gelfand Rennert & Feldman
1880 Century Park E., Ste. 900
Los Angeles, California 90067

Nyrraw (ASCAP)
see EMI Music Publishing

O

O/B/O Itself and Estes Park (BMI)
see MCA Music

O-Tex Music (BMI)
see Zomba Music

Obverse Creation Music (ASCAP)
see Sony ATV Music

Of Music (ASCAP)
see PolyGram Records Inc.

Old Crow (BMI)
10585 Santa Monica Blvd.
Los Angeles, California 90025

On the Fox (BMI)
see McLaughlin Publishing Co.

On the Mantel (BMI)
see Acuff Rose Music

One Big Love (ASCAP)
see Polygram Music Publishing Inc.

1972 Music (SESAC)
see EMI Music Publishing

Only Hit Music (BMI)
see MCA Music

Organized Noize
Address Unavailable

P

Pan for Gold (BMI)
see Copyright Management Inc.

Paradise American Style (BMI)
see Warner-Chappell Music

Parker Pen (BMI)
see EMI Music Publishing

Pearl White (BMI)
see EMI Music Publishing

Peer Pera (ASCAP)
see EMI Music Publishing

Peer-Southern Organization (ASCAP)
810 7th Ave.
New York, New York 10019

Pener Pig (BMI)
see Polygram Music Publishing Inc.

Perfect Songs Music (BMI)
see EMI Music Publishing

Pie Eyed Groobie (ASCAP)
see Groobee

Piercepettisongs Music (ASCAP)
see Polygram Music Publishing Inc.

Pink Smoke Music (BMI)
see EMI Music Publishing

Polygram International Music (ASCAP)
1416 N. LaBrea Ave.
Los Angeles, California 90028

Polygram Music Publishing Inc. (ASCAP)
Attn: Brian Kelleher
c/o Polygram Records Inc.
810 7th Ave.
New York, New York 10019

PolyGram Records Inc. (ASCAP)
810 7th Ave.
New York, New York 10019

List of Publishers

Pomus (BMI)
see Warner-Chappell Music

Price is Right Music (ASCAP)
see MCA Music

Puckalesia (BMI)
see Warner-Chappell Music

Pure Love (ASCAP)
see Warner-Chappell Music

Q

Quartet Music, Inc. (ASCAP)
1619 Broadway
New York, New York 10019

Quinlan Road (SESAC)
see Warner-Chappell Music

R

Ranch Rock (ASCAP)
see Warner-Chappell Music

Realsongs (ASCAP)
Attn: Diane Warren
6363 Sunset Blvd., Ste. 810
Hollywood, California 90028

Red Brazos (BMI)
Box 163870
Austin, Texas 78716

Louise Red (BMI)
see Windswept Pacific

Rella Music Corp. (BMI)
see Warner-Chappell Music

Remarkable (ASCAP)
see Warner-Chappell Music

Rezlee (ASCAP)
see EMI Music Publishing

Ri Ho (BMI)
see Polygram Music Publishing Inc.

Rickety Raw (ASCAP)
see EMI Music Publishing

Righteous Babe Music (BMI)
P. O. Box 95, Ellicott Station
Buffalo, New York 14205

Ring Musik
Address Unavailable

Rio Bravo Music (BMI)
see Major Bob Music

Toni Robi Music (ASCAP)
see 2000 Watts Music

Rock Candy (ASCAP)
see EMI Music Publishing

Rock and Roll Credit Card (BMI)
see Dreamworks

Rodali (ASCAP)
see Sony ATV Music

Rodney Jerkins Music (BMI)
see EMI Music Publishing

Romanesque (ASCAP)
see Warner-Chappell Music

Rondor Music Inc. (ASCAP)
see Almo Music Corp.

Rounder Music (ASCAP)
1 Camp St.
Cambridge, Massachusetts 02140

Ruff Ryders (ASCAP)
see Boomer X

Ruthensmear (BMI)
see EMI Music Publishing

Rutland Road (ASCAP)
see WB Music

Rye Songs (BMI)
see Sony ATV Music

RZO (BMI)
see EMI Music Publishing

S

Sa (ASCAP)
97 Croft Ln.
Smithtown, New York 11787

Salzillo (BMI)
see Red Brazos

Sanga Music Inc. (BMI)
250 W. 57th St., Ste. 2017
New York, New York 10019

Scrap Metal Music (BMI)
see EMI Music Publishing

Screen Gems-EMI Music Inc. (BMI)
6255 Sunset Blvd., 12th Fl.
Hollywood, California 90028

Scrogrow Music (BMI)
see Warner-Chappell Music

Seasons Four Music Corp. (BMI)
see Gavadima Music Inc.

7 Mary Three Music (BMI)
see EMI Music Publishing

Seven Summits (BMI)
see Starstruck Writers Group

Seventh Son Music (ASCAP)
Box 158717
Nashville, Tennessee 37215

Sharondipity (ASCAP)
see MCA Music

Sharoonie (BMI)
see Warner-Chappell Music

Sheek Louchion Music (BMI)
see EMI Music Publishing

Richard Shindell Music (ASCAP)
c/o Young/Hunter Mgmt.
65 East St., PO Box 303
Chesterfield, Massachusetts 08012

Showbilly (BMI)
see Sony ATV Tree Publishing

Mort Shuman (BMI)
see Warner-Chappell Music

Sidungpoint (SOCAN)
Address Unavailable

Paul Simon Music (BMI)
1619 Broadway
New York, New York 10019

Singing River Publishing Co., Inc. (BMI)
c/o Marion Carpenter
205 Acacia St.
Biloxi, Mississippi 39530

Single's Only (BMI)
see EMI Music Publishing

Siquomb Publishing Corp. (BMI)
c/o Segel & Goldman Inc.
9348 Santa Monica Blvd.
Beverly Hills, California 90210

Sixteen Stars Music (BMI)
see Dixie Stars Music

Skinny White Butt (ASCAP)
see Warner-Chappell Music

Slack A. D. Music (ASCAP)
see EMI Music Publishing

Slam U Well Music (BMI)
see Warner-Chappell Music

Slav Tu Tu Five (BMI)
see Almo/Irving Music

Smash Vegas (ASCAP)
see EMI Music Publishing

SMB (ASCAP)
see Windswept Pacific

Smelzgood (ASCAP)
1642 E. 56th St.
Chicago, Illinois 60637

Smokin' for Lifewarner (BMI)
see Chappell & Co., Inc.

List of Publishers

Snowden Music (ASCAP)
Box 11512th St.
Purdys, New York 10578

So So Def Music (ASCAP)
see EMI Music Publishing

Song Island Music (BMI)
see EMI Music Publishing

Song Matters Music (ASCAP)
see Ensign Music

Songs of Golgotha (BMI)
see Dinger & Ollie Music

Songs of Polygram (BMI)
see Polygram International Music

Sony ATV Cross Keys Publishing Co. Inc.
c/o Donna Hilley
PO Box 1273
Nashville, Tennessee 37202

Sony ATV Music (ASCAP)
550 Madison Ave.
New York, New York 10022

Sony ATV Songs (BMI)
see Sony ATV Music

Sony ATV Tree Publishing (BMI)
1111 16th Ave. S.
Nashville, Tennessee 37212

Sounds of Da Red Drum (ASCAP)
see Almo/Irving Music

Southfield Road (ASCAP)
Address Unavailable

Southwind Music, Inc. (BMI)
c/o John M. Weaver
739 E. Main St.
Ventura, California 93001

Special Rider Music (SESAC)
PO Box 860, Cooper Sta.
New York, New York 10276

Spent Bullets Music
see BMG Music

Larry Spier, Inc. (ASCAP)
928 Broadway, Ste. 205
New York, New York 10010

M. Spiro (BMI)
see Acuff Rose Music

Springalo Toones (BMI)
7715 Sunset Blvd., Ste. 200
Los Angeles, California 90046

Mark Alan Springer Music (BMI)
see EMI Music Publishing

Bruce Springsteen Publishing (ASCAP)
c/o Jon Landau Management, Inc.
Attn: Barbara Carr
136 E. 57th St., No. 1202
New York, New York 10021

Springtime Music Inc. (BMI)
c/o Andrew Feinman
424 Madison Ave.
New York, New York 10017

Spur66 (SESAC)
see Famous Music Corp.

SPZ (BMI)
see EMI Music Publishing

Stamen (BMI)
see EMI Music Publishing

Stapp/Tremonti Music (BMI)
c/o Wind Up Records
72 Madison Ave.
New York, New York 10016

Starstruck Angel Music (BMI)
see Starstruck Writers Group

Starstruck Writers Group (ASCAP)
PO Box 121996
Nashville, Tennessee 37212

Steady Mobbin' (BMI)
see EMI Music Publishing

Jeff Stevens Music (BMI)
see Warner-Chappell Music

List of Publishers

Still Working for the Man Music (BMI)
see Sony ATV Music

Stingray Sounds (ASCAP)
see EMI Music Publishing

Mike Stoller Music (ASCAP)
9000 Sunset Blvd.
Ste. 1107
Los Angeles, California 90069

Stone Agate Music (ASCAP)
see Jobete Music Co.

Stone Diamond Music (BMI)
see Jobete Music Co.

Storm Hymnal Music (BMI)
c/o Siegel, et al
10345 Santa Monica Blvd.
Los Angeles, California 90025

Strange Mind Productions (ASCAP)
see MCA, Inc.

Stratford Music Corp. (ASCAP)
see Chappell & Co., Inc.

Streamline Moderne (BMI)
see Warner-Chappell Music

Strictly TQ (ASCAP)
see EMI Music Publishing

Studio Nomado Music (BMI)
see Sony ATV Music

Tom Sturges (ASCAP)
see Chrysalis Music Group

Succubus Music (ASCAP)
see Warner-Chappell Music

Suge Music (BMI)
see Sony ATV Music

Keith Sweat Publishing (ASCAP)
c/o Gelfano, Rennert & Feldman
1301 Avenue of the Americas, 8th Fl
.
New York, New York 10019

Sword and Stone Music (ASCAP)
10209 Gary Rd.
Potomac, Maryland 20854

Keith Sykes Music (BMI)
c/o Keith Sykes
3974 Hawkins Mill Rd.
Memphis, Tennessee 38128

T

T-Boy Music (ASCAP)
c/o Lipservices
1841 Broadway, Ste. 411
New York, New York 10023

Talmont Music Co. (BMI)
c/o Pickwick International
1370 Avenue of the Americas, Ste. 6
New York, New York 10019

Samuel Taylor (ASCAP)
see Boomer X

TCF (ASCAP)
see WB Music

TCF Music (ASCAP)
see Warner-Chappell Music

Te Bass (BMI)
see EMI Music Publishing

Teapot Music (ASCAP)
c/o Bobby Whiteside Ltd.
100 E. Walton St.
Chicago, Illinois 60611

Temporary Music (BMI)
see Warner-Chappell Music

Ten-East Music (BMI)
c/o L. Lee Phillips
Mitchell, Silberberg & Knupp
1800 Century Park, E.
Los Angeles, California 90067

Terilee Music (BMI)
see Sony ATV Tree Publishing

List of Publishers

Terri Ooo (ASCAP)
see Polygram Music Publishing Inc.

Tesh (BMI)
c/o Steve Calas & Assoc.
12424 Wilshire Blvd., Ste. 1150
Los Angeles, California

Tete San Ko Music (ASCAP)
see Sony ATV Music

Texas Wedge Music (ASCAP)
37 Music Sq. E
Nashville, Tennessee 37203

Them Young Boys (ASCAP)
see Bug Music

3EB Music (BMI)
see EMI Music Publishing

Throwin' Tantrums Music (ASCAP)
see EMI Music Publishing

Tickson Music (BMI)
see Len Freedman Music

Time for Flytes Music (BMI)
see EMI Music Publishing

TJ (ASCAP)
see EMI Music Publishing

Tokeco Music (BMI)
see Polygram Music Publishing Inc.

Tol Muziek (BMI)
see EMI Music Publishing

Tommy Jymi, Inc. (BMI)
c/o Dennis Katz, Esq.
845 3rd Ave.
New York, New York 10022

Transmission/God is Greater (ASCAP)
833 W. Buena, Apt. 1102
Chicago, Illinois 60613

Treat Baker Music (SOCAN)
c/o NGB Inc.
579 Richmond St. W., Ste. 401
Toronto, Ontario M5V1Y6
Canada

Tree Publishing Co., Inc. (BMI)
see Sony ATV Tree Publishing

Treyball Music (ASCAP)
see Sony ATV Music

Trio Music Co., Inc. (BMI)
c/o Leiber & Stoller
9000 Sunset Blvd., Ste. 1107
Los Angeles, California 90069

TRO-Folkways Music Publishers, Inc. (BMI)
10 Columbus Circle, Ste. 1460
New York, New York 10019

Trottsky Music (BMI)
see Warner-Chappell Music

Trumpet Blast Music (BMI)
see Bug Music

Turgid Tunes (BMI)
see Bug Music

Twelve & Under Music (ASCAP)
see EMI Music Publishing

Twentieth Century-Fox Music Corp. (ASCAP)
Attn: Herbert N. Eiseman
PO Box 900
Beverly Hills, California 90213

Twin Creeks (ASCAP)
see Almo/Irving Music

2000 Watts Music (ASCAP)
c/o Darrell Allanby
375 Mt. Prospect Ave.
Newark, New Jersey 07104

Tyde (BMI)
see Sony ATV Music

Tyland Music (BMI)
see EMI Music Publishing

T'Ziah's Music (BMI)
see EMI Music Publishing

U

Unart Music Corp. (BMI)
see United Artists Music Co., Inc.

Underachiever Music (BMI)
23564 Calabasas Rd., Ste. 107
Calabasas, California 91302

Unichappell Music Inc. (BMI)
see Warner-Chappell Music

United Artists Music Co., Inc.
6753 Hollywood Blvd.
Los Angeles, California 90028

Untertainment (ASCAP)
see Warner-Chappell Music

UR IV Music (ASCAP)
see EMI Music Publishing

Urban Warfare (ASCAP)
see Warner-Chappell Music

V

Valet (BMI)
2442 NW Market St., Ste. 273
Seattle, Washington 98107

Vallallen (ASCAP)
see Black Lava

Phil Vassar (ASCAP)
see EMI Music Publishing

Vibe Crusher Music (BMI)
see Almo/Irving

Vibzelect (BMI)
see Sony ATV Music

Virgin Music (ASCAP)
see EMI Music Publishing

Virginia Beach Music (ASCAP)
see Warner-Chappell Music

VLS (ASCAP)
c/o Feinstein Management
120 E. 34th St., Pent. B
New York, New York 10016

W

Wacissa River Music (BMI)
1102 17th Ave. S., Ste. 400
Nashville, Tennessee 37212

Wally World (ASCAP)
see Warner-Chappell Music

Wanted Woman (BMI)
see Red Brazos

War Bride Music (BMI)
see EMI Music Publishing

Steve Wariner (BMI)
c/o Siren Songs
Gelfand, Rennert & Feldman
1880 Century Park, E., No. 900
Los Angeles, California 90067

Warner-Chappell Music (ASCAP)
10585 Santa Monica Blvd.
Los Angeles, California 90025

Warner-Tamerlane Music (BMI)
see Warner-Chappell Music

Warren G Music (ASCAP)
see EMI Music Publishing

Diane Warren Trust (ASCAP)
see Realsongs

Chris Waters Music
Address Unavailable

WB Music (ASCAP)
10585 Santa Monica Blvd.
Los Angeles, California 90025

Stan Webb (SESAC)
see Bug Music

Webo Girl (ASCAP)
see House of Fun Music

Wedgewood Avenue Music (BMI)
see Windswept Pacific

Weetie Pie
see Polygram Music Publishing Inc.

List of Publishers

Welsh Witch Publishing (BMI)
c/o Gelfand, Breslauer, Rennert & F
1800 Century Park E., Ste. 900
Los Angeles, California 90067

When It Raines (BMI)
see BMG Music

Wiggly Tooth Music (ASCAP)
see Warner-Chappell Music

Wild Country Music (BMI)
see Warner-Chappell Music

Wildawn Music (ASCAP)
see Teapot Music

Will K (BMI)
see MCA Music

Darron Williams (ASCAP)
see EMI Music Publishing

Williamson Music (ASCAP)
see Warner-Chappell Music

Windswept (BMI)
see Windswept Pacific

Windswept Pacific (ASCAP)
4450 Lakeside Dr., Ste. 200
Burbank, California 91505

Wish Bone (ASCAP)
see Sony ATV Music

Withrow Publishing (ASCAP)
see MCA, Inc.

Wixen Music (BMI)
see Warner-Chappell Music

Wiz (BMI)
see EMI Music Publishing

Wonderland Music (BMI)
see Walt Disney Music

Woolnough Music Inc. (BMI)
1550 Neptune
Leucadia, California 92024

World Pacific (BMI)
see Windswept Pacific

Write Treatage Music (ASCAP)
207 1/2 1st Ave. S.
Seattle, Washington 98104

Wu-Tang Music (BMI)
see BMG Music

Y

Yab Yum (BMI)
see Sony ATV Music

Yah Mo Publishing (BMI)
c/o Debra Ingram
867 Muirfield Rd.
Los Angeles, California 90005

Yah Yah Music (ASCAP)
see EMI Music Publishing

Yam Gruel Music (ASCAP)
see Arzo Music

Yes Dear (BMI)
see Bug Music

Z

Zadiyah's (BMI)
see Windswept Pacific

Zargon (ASCAP)
c/o Breslauer, Jacobson, Rutman, &
10345 Olympic Blvd.
Los Angeles, California 90064

Zevon Music Inc. (BMI)
c/o Jess Morgan & Co., Inc.
6420 Wilshire Blvd., 19th Fl.
Los Angeles, California 90048

Zomba House (ASCAP)
137-139 W. 25th St, 8th Floor
New York, New York 10001

Zomba Music (ASCAP)
137-139 W. 25th St., 8th Fl.
New York, New York 10001

ISBN 0-7876-1507-2

90000